FLYING ALASKA AFTER 50

Some Skill, Some Luck, Always Interesting

GARY S. EVANS

KENMORE, WA

Epicenter Press

6524 NE 181st St., Suite 2, Kenmore, WA 98028

Epicenter Press is a regional press publishing nonfiction books about the arts, history, environment, and diverse cultures and lifestyles of Alaska and the Pacific Northwest. For more information, visit www.EpicenterPress.com

Flying Alaska After 50
Copyright © 2026 by Gary S. Evans

No generative AI was used in the conceptualization, planning, drafting, or creative writing of this work. No permission is given for the use of this material for AI training purposes.

All rights reserved. No part of this publication may be reproduced, stored in a retrieval system, or transmitted in any form by any means, electronic, mechanical, photocopying, recording, or otherwise, without the prior written permission of the publisher. Permission is given for brief excerpts to be published with book reviews in newspaper, magazines, newsletters, catalogs, and online publications.

Cover design: Scott Book
Interior design: Melissa Vail Coffman

Library of Congress Control Number: 2025942371

ISBN: 978-1-684922-83-3 (Trade Paperback)
ISBN: 978-1-684922-84-0 (Ebook)

This book is dedicated to all the pilots in my family who repeatedly told me "You should write a book!"

Acknowledgments . . . . *ix*
Foreword . . . . *xi*

CHAPTER I

Introduction – The Homer Years 1
Bull at Perl Island 2
Valdez Oil Spill 4
Fuel Dumb and Happy 5
Balancing Act 8
Magneto Mambo 9
Fog at Anchorage 11
An Inch is as Good as a Mile 13
A Knock in the Night 14

CHAPTER II

St Mary's – Bethel Area 17
Spaghetti and Meatballs 19
Star Light, Star Bright 20
Bethel Blues 21
Life Flight to Bethel 23

CHAPTER III

Cold Bay 25
Ice Over Belkofski Bay 26
Murphy's Law (If it can go wrong . . .). 29
Poem: Life Flight to King Cove 31
False Pass Fiasco. 33
Life Flight from Port Moller 35
Motor Man. 48
Bear Tales. 41
    At the Window 41
    Shopping for Groceries. 41
    The Whale at Navy Town 42
    Fishing for Silvers. 42
    Bear at the Foot Bridge. 43
    Adrenaline Rush 43
    Surprise at the Hanger Door. 44
    Juneau Lake 44
Perryville Pee-In. 46
Stuck Again in Cold Bay 47
Unscheduled Landing. 48
Poem: Life Flight from Bear Lake 50
Prince Bandar Bear Hunt. 51

CHAPTER IV

Caravan at Aniakchak. 55
Ice Again 58
Almost Exhausted 59
A Propane High 61
Danger of No Smoking 63

Going to the Dogs. 65
Runway Incursion. 66
Category III in a Cessna 207 67
Special Request 70
Crash at King Salmon. 71
Taylorcraft Restoration 74
Evans Mosquito 77

My 10 Rules for Flying the Bush. 79
Glossary. 81

ACKNOWLEDGMENTS

I WANT TO THANK MY WIFE, LOA, also a pilot, for her unwavering support and encouragement, without which I may never have finished this work. She typed my drafts interpreting my longhand, and gave valuable advice on editing and polishing my stories.

I also want to thank our dear friend, Diane D., for her faithful assistance with editing and completing all the formatting of this material to the publisher's specifications. She is a mover and shaker whose encouragement also spurred me on to complete this book.

This book is dedicated to all the pilots in my family who repeatedly told me, "You should write a book!"

FOREWORD

I BEGAN COMMERCIAL FLYING LATE, WHEN I was 52 years old. Construction in Anchorage, Alaska, had gone bust in the late 1980s, so I closed down my small general contracting company and was looking for something to do. I decided to look for a job flying for one of the small Part 135 airlines operating in the state. I had the ratings and I liked to fly. I knew that, at my age, I would not move up to flying larger aircraft. Flying small bush type airplanes would be more fun, and it still is.

At the time I started commercial flying, my plan was to resume my general contracting company when the Alaskan economy improved. However, after I was able to rescue people with very serious medical emergencies in dangerous weather conditions, I changed my mind. I realized there may be a higher purpose in life than making money. Maybe I was where I needed to be.

Some of the stories related here might lead the reader to believe that flying small planes in Alaska is a dangerous thing to do, and I suppose statistics bear that out. Except for a few medical emergency flights, that was not necessarily the case. These stories occurred over a period of thirteen-and-a-half years and more than 15,000 hours of flight time.

Many of these hours were flown in high winds, rain, snow, and fog over remote and mountainous country. We flew passengers, freight, and mail to the villages and hunters and fishermen to lodges and remote camps. We landed on makeshift gravel and dirt strips. None of the thousands of passengers I flew ever got a scratch.

Except for emergency life flights, which I never turned down, my philosophy while flying has always been if there is any doubt about the outcome of the operation, then you do not do it. Of course the more you do something the more skilled you become and the more you can do. In the 15,000 plus hours I flew the bush, I averaged more than two take-offs and landings per hour—which adds up to about 30,000.

Chapter I

Introduction – The Homer Years

My first commercial flying job was with CIA. No, not that one, Cook Inlet Aviation. CIA was a small Part 135 airline that was based in Homer, Alaska on Kachemak Bay. Kachemak Bay is a very beautiful area, made famous by Tom Bodett's radio broadcast "The End of the Road" and the Kilcher family's television show "Alaska, the Last Frontier."

Cook Inlet Aviation's fleet of airplanes included a Cessna 172, 185, two 207's, a Piper Aztec, and a DeHavilland Single Otter. We flew passengers, freight, and mail to the native villages of Port Graham and English Bay and the small fishing town of Seldovia. We also flew passengers and freight to the head of Kachemak Bay, where the Bradley Lake Dam was under construction. CIA had the contract to carry UPS packages between Homer and Anchorage five days a week. During the summer months, we flew tourists over the Harding Ice Fields and the Kenai Fjords. Most of the flying was routine, however a few incidents were not.

The Bull at Perl Island

One day, I was sent on a charter to Perl Island with a Cessna 207 to pick up a couple who were moving off the island along with some of their goods and chattel. Perl Island is very remote and they were the only inhabitants, aside from the wild cattle that thrived there due to the lack of predators, such as wolves or bears. The Island was named after Perl Blodgett, a man who came to the island in 1883.

The airline owner told me there was no airstrip on the island, but to look for a worn strip in the grass of what used to be a pasture. The pasture would be located near the only buildings on the island. I made my way the 50 miles out past Dangerous Cape, English Bay, and Elizabeth Island to Perl Island. I could see the ground below, but the so-called landing strip was not readily apparent and I spent a few minutes milling around looking for it. I picked out what I thought it might be and took a second look. Once sure of it, I made my approach from out over the water. The strip was very narrow with a dog leg turn in the middle of it. Naturally there was a strong cross wind but I managed to touch down right where I wanted.

The ground was unbelievably rough with humps and dips. Fortunately, the 207 had a heavy-duty nose gear, but it was taking a beating. I made the dog leg turn and was rolling out when I noticed a huge brindle colored bull that had been standing off to the side. He was not pleased and looked like he wanted to charge.

I taxied down to the end of the strip where I could see my passengers waiting with a pile of boxes. I wheeled the plane around and saw the bull had gone back to eating grass. I began loading the boxes and found that many of them were filled with books. With the amount of fuel on board, and considering the size of the passengers, I was concerned about the length and condition of the strip. The strip was very narrow, not as wide as the wingspan of the plane. The dog leg turned to the right and the crosswind was coming from the right. I knew I would have to keep the nose up to avoid damaging the nose gear.

The Cessna 207 has a long nose and a high instrument panel,

and it was going to be difficult to see when to turn at the bend in the strip. The grass on both sides was high and I would need to stay centered. I was getting ready to tie things down when the man said "Just a minute." He went into one of the buildings and came out with a huge white dog. I shuffled things around and, finally, everything and everybody was buckled in and the doors were closed. The man was sitting in the co-pilot seat with the dog sitting behind him like a person. The woman was sitting behind me. Of the three, I liked the dog the best.

Once I had given my briefing about seat belts, no smoking, door handles, and survival gear, etc. I started the engine, checked the mags and prop, and contemplated the situation. I selected 20 degrees of flaps, set the trim, checked fuel to the proper tank, and turned to aim down the strip.

The bull was 150 feet to the side of the strip, still eating grass. I adjusted the mixture for full power, firewalled the throttle, and released the brakes. As we bumped and banged down the strip, I concentrated on holding the nose up while keeping the right amount of aileron into the wind—intent on watching for the dog leg turn. Just as we were coming to it there was a bloodcurdling scream behind me, and the dog started barking.

I looked about wildly and quickly saw the problem. The bull was charging. He had his head down, his tail up, and he was coming hard. He was close but turned away at the last moment. By then we were floundering through the tall grass. I put down full flaps and the old 207 staggered into the air. With the stall warning moaning we were just able to clear an old rusty barbed wire fence and dive for the beach to gain flying speed. When I finally got myself organized with flaps up and the throttle and prop set for normal climb, I noticed air rushing in the cabin. I looked around to see what was happening and saw that the woman had put her elbow through the Plexiglas side window. Nothing I could do about that, except get to Homer as soon as possible with the breeze blowing in.

After we landed, the passengers never said a word. They

collected the freight and the dog and paid the bill. When they had gone, I examined the airplane. The propeller was green, large bunches of grass were hanging from the landing gear, and there was a big smear of manure down the side. I cleaned the plane up and that evening and we replaced the Plexiglas window with material we had in the shop.

I decided I would not take the 207 into the Super Cub strip at Perl Island again and made my first of 10 rules for flying in the bush: if there is any doubt about the outcome of an operation, then do not do it.

Valdez Oil Spill

The Valdez oil spill occurred in March of 1989 when the oil tanker, Exxon Valdez, fetched up on Bligh Reef, spilling 11 million gallons of crude oil into Prince William Sound near the city of Valdez, Alaska. The ship's captain, Hazelwood, had been drinking and left the bridge in charge of an inexperienced third mate. That mistake cost Exxon Oil Company 2.5 billion dollars and did untold damage to the environment.

After the spill happened, there was an all-out effort to clean up the oil. Crews were doing all they could to clean up the beaches that were affected. Many small boats and inflatable Zodiac type boats were required. There was a need for a lot of small boat anchors, and Cook Inlet Aviation was chartered to take a collection of them from Homer, Alaska to Valdez on an emergency basis.

We had enough anchors to fill up the single engine De Havilland Otter and the Cessna 207 to gross weight. We needed to deliver them overnight from Homer on a direct flight the 204 miles over the Harding Ice Fields, the Chugach Mountains, then the Gulf of Alaska and Prince William Sound to Valdez.

The company owner took off first in the single Otter and I followed flying the 207. The first part of the flight would be IFR after we passed Seward, but would improve and clear up approaching

Valdez. It was a moonless night, and I did not like the idea of flying IFR over wild, mountainous country and then over the open water of the Gulf of Alaska and Prince William Sound in the middle of the night. The 207 was old and tired and with the heavy load its performance was not good.

About halfway out over the water the engine temps began to creep up. I enriched the fuel mixture and opened the cowl flaps and eased the power back. The temperatures stabilized, although still higher than normal. I knew that an engine failure would be fatal. Finally, way out in the distance, I saw the lights of Valdez.

When I arrived at Valdez the runway lights were all on and it was easy to get lined up and make the approach. There was no other traffic so I continued on down. At about one half mile and 200 feet high, all the runway lights suddenly went out. I was able to land, taxied to the ramp, and parked next to the Otter, glad to be done with the flight.

On the way back to Homer the next morning, I circled around to be overland most of the way.

Fuel Dumb and Happy

Cook Inlet Aviation also had a contract with UPS to carry packages from Anchorage to Homer five days a week. We had to leave Homer early so we could get back in time to deliver them to the UPS agent by ten o'clock in the morning. We used either the Single Otter or the Cessna 207 depending on the load. On this particular morning, it was the 207. I filled the long range tanks with 80 gallons of gas and secured the caps, planning to use one tank going to Anchorage and the other tank on the return. There should be half tanks remaining when I got back.

The weather was beautiful, and the Anchorage approach got me lined up to runway 6R without delay. When the truck came with the packages, I had my doubts it would all fit. I loaded and unloaded the plane twice before finding the combination to get them all in. I got my clearance and was soon on my way across Turnagain Arm. It was a blue-sky day, and I remember thinking how lucky I was to actually be paid for doing this. It is a beautiful area and I liked flying there.

I flew down along the mountains past Skilak Lake and then over the end of Tustumena Lake. From there, I cut across the low area where they were building a power line from the new dam at Bradley Lake, at the head of Kachemak Bay toward Kenai. I noticed the left tank I was using was showing slightly low, but dismissed it as a problem with the fuel gauge sending float. I had personally filled the tanks and secured the caps, so there had to be a little more than half a tank remaining.

As I neared Homer, I started letting down, and was at about 700 feet when I contacted Homer Flight Service to check for traffic. I notified them of my intention to make a straight in approach to runway 21. Just beyond Stone Step Lake, the engine quit without warning. I pushed the mixture control all the way in and hit the boost pump. There was no response from the engine, so I left the pump on and switched tanks.

A loaded 207 at 700 feet is on the ground in about a minute. There was still no response from the engine, so I called Flight Service and told them I had a failed engine and was going to try for the beach. Fortunately, the tide was out, and there was a good looking area ahead if I could reach it. I pulled the prop control back to increase the gliding distance and it looked good except for two large boulders that I would not clear. I saw that if I turned out over the water I could go between them and make a skidding turn down the beach. When I knew I had it made, I put down full flaps and turned everything off. I touched down right at the water's edge, and was able to make the turn without damage. I turned on the master switch long enough to raise the flaps and attempt to call Flight Service. There was no answer, so I got out and began stacking the UPS packages above the tide line, where they would be safe.

Just then, the owner of the company came over, flying the Cessna 185. He had heard my call to Flight Service. He was giving a check ride to one of the other pilots. The 185 had large tires, so he was able to circle and land the other way. The owner and the other pilot helped finish moving the packages. When we had them all safe, we checked out the 207. The tank I had been using was empty and the other one was half full. A little more with the boost pump and the engine started.

The area we had to takeoff from was very short and was getting narrower by the minute because the tide was coming in. The owner told me, "You ride with the other pilot and I will see if I can get the 207 out." On takeoff, the 185 pilot was distracted because he had forgotten to set the trim. He got one wheel in the water and there was water spraying clear over the wing. We managed to get into the air and turned to watch the 207 takeoff. It looked like he was way too slow but he cleared the rocks by inches.

When we got back to the hangar, we examined the 207 more closely, and discovered fuel stains on the left stabilizer. The seal where the fuel filler is attached to the fuel bladder neck had failed and allowed the fuel to siphon out on the way to Anchorage and return. The bottom of the fuel bladder had been sucked up against the fuel level sending float, so that the tank gauge was showing nearly half full. I learned that timing the fuel burn from a known quantity is not a guarantee. I should have switched to the tank with the gauge showing the correct amount. I will not make that mistake again.

The owner chartered a helicopter to retrieve the packages and we got them delivered on time. The FAA let the whole thing go because there were no passengers and there was no damage. And, it is legal to land on the beach in Alaska.

BALANCING ACT

Shortly after I started flying for Cook Inlet Aviation, I needed to get checked out in the DeHavilland Single Otter. I was to fly as co-pilot on a trip to Port Graham with a heavy load of freight for the village store. I had just come in from a sightseeing flight over the Harding Ice Field, so I was not around when the Otter was loaded. The calculations showed that we would be right at gross weight for the trip. The DeHavilland Otter is a big plane, as far as single engine planes go. It will take off and land on very short strips with a heavy load. It is noisy and slow, and the only plane that I have ever flown that, if you have the power up and what seems like the nose down, it will climb like an elevator.

We checked to see that everything was tied down and started the engine. We let it warm up until all the temperatures and pressures were in the green, and taxied out for takeoff. The owner of the company was flying, and he elected to make an intersection takeoff using only part of the runway. The thought crossed my mind that with this heavy load, we should be using more of it; but I figured that he had been flying the Otter for a long time, and I wasn't even checked out in it, so I said nothing.

The takeoff roll was longer than I thought was normal, but we lifted off right at the end. I was looking out for traffic when I heard an exclamation on the intercom. I turned and saw him rolling the trim. He said, "Check this out!" The control column was full forward against the stop. We still had 10 degrees of flaps with takeoff power. We had no way to get the nose down in case of a stall. He began a very shallow, coordinated turn back to the airport.

The flaps on the Otter are hydraulically operated. One sets the selector either up or down and then pumps a handle between the seats to operate them. When we finally got back around and lined up on final approach, he made sure the selector indicated down and told me to grab the flap handle but to do nothing unless he yelled or we started to stall. In that case, I was to pump as hard and fast as I could. It turned out that he was able to carefully adjust the power on the ragged edge of a stall and get down. We hit tail first, and the mains banged down hard, but there was no damage.

When we got back to the ramp we found out that the ramp guys had placed a large load of soda pop behind the rear bulkhead of the cabin. This caused a very tail heavy condition. It was amazing that the Otter would fly so out of balance.

After that experience, I have never flown an airplane without knowing how it was loaded. I added that to my 10 rules for flying in the bush.

Gary Evans with Single Otter

Magneto Mambo

One day we waited all morning for the fog to lift, so we could make the mail run to Seldovia, English Bay, and Port Graham. Finally, about noon, the fog lifted to our company minimums of a 500 foot ceiling and two miles visibility. I was already loaded, and when the ATIS announced those conditions, I headed across Kachemak Bay in one of the Cessna 207s.

My last stop was at Port Graham. When I had unloaded the mail, there were four passengers who wanted to go to Homer. So I put up four seats and made sure the seatbelts were snapped in correctly. I got the passengers loaded along with their baggage and gave my briefing about seat belts, no smoking, locations of the fire extinguisher and door handles, etc.

Just as I was ready to start the engine, a fellow came up and said he wanted to go. I could see that he was staggering drunk, so I told him he could not go. He walked away a little but, as soon as he heard the fuel pump come on, he ran over and hugged the prop and said he wanted to go. I got out and pulled him away from the prop and told him, with a few choice words, that he could not go. When I went to start the engine, he ran over and did it again. I got on the radio and asked our village agent to have the VPSO come. We waited about 10 minutes before the officer finally came riding up in his four wheeler to take care of the situation.

The gravel runway at Port Graham is 1,975 feet long with a hill 700 feet off the end of runway 12 and a stand of trees 1,000 feet off the end of runway 30. The wind favored runway 30, so I taxied to the run-up area. I checked the magnetos and prop governor, fuel to the proper tank, trim set, and flaps to ten degrees. I made sure all seat belts were fastened and checked for traffic. I rolled out on runway 30 and firewalled the throttle. All was normal, and we lifted off in about 1400 feet.

As we were coming to the trees, the engine began to shake and run very rough, and I could see that we would not clear the tree line. Fortunately, there was an area off to the side that opened out to the water with a small sand beach. I aimed for that and did a magneto check. When I turned to the right mag, the engine quit completely. When I turned to the left mag, the engine ran smoothly with almost normal power.

I continued on around to Seldovia where we had a small shack with a phone and called the company. They sent the other 207 to take the passengers. When we examined the offending mag, we discovered that the internal gear had stripped some teeth and caused it to fire erratically. We put on a replacement mag, and when I got back to Homer, I was ready for lunch, and a little more.

It worked out well, but from that time until now, I have always taken a moment to think about what I will do on every takeoff if the engine fails.

Fog at Anchorage

One evening, after flying the regular schedule and a sightseeing trip over the Kenai Fjords, I was asked to take the company Cessna 172 to Anchorage that evening to pick up two fishermen. They had chartered an early morning flight to Homer. They were going out to a lodge for a guided fishing week they had booked on the Kenai River. That would work out well, because I could stay at my home on Mirror Lake near Anchorage, and be ready to pick them up at Anchorage International Airport early in the morning.

I filled the fuel tanks to the brim and checked the Anchorage weather. The report was CAVU (ceiling and visibility unlimited). The flight to Anchorage was very smooth. The moon was shining on the mountains, and I had some nice music playing on the ADF. About 20 miles from Anchorage, I tuned in the AWOS and was surprised to hear that fog had rolled in. Conditions were being reported as 400 foot ceiling with a half mile visibility. I contacted Anchorage approach and requested an ILS to runway 6L. Visibility had remained good until I neared Anchorage.

I contacted Anchorage tower and was cleared for the approach. The fog started at the outer marker on Fire Island. I reported the outer marker and started down the ILS. At the missed approach point I could see nothing and had to declare a missed approach. I flew the missed approach procedure and climbed back up above the fog layer. The tower advised me that the visibility might be better on the approach to 24R, so I went on around for the localizer approach. For a while, I could see the traffic on International Boulevard and it looked like I would make it. Unfortunately, the visibility went to zero and I had to declare another missed approach. After flying the missed approach, I notified the tower that I was going to go out to Birchwood, close to my home, and try there.

Upon arriving at Birchwood, I found it fogged in. I called Elmendorf Air Force Base and the report was fog to the ground. I requested a GCA (ground control approach), but they were unable because the equipment was out of service. The week before I had landed a Piper J-5 Cub on a very short, steep, and rough strip on a mountain top near Flattop Mountain at Anchorage. An attempt to land there in a Cessna 172 at night would almost certainly result in wrecking the aircraft. I dismissed that option. I called Flight Service and requested the weather at Palmer, Wasilla, Kenai, and Soldotna. They were all fogged in, but Homer was still reporting in the clear.

I carefully calculated the time I had been in the air. I had been flying leaned out to best economy cruise, except for the two ILS missed approaches. There was no wind, so I rechecked my calculations. The 172 had a 180 horse power engine and a constant speed propeller. I should have just enough fuel to get back to Homer, so I notified Flight Service of my intentions. I leaned the mixture, pulled the prop back as much as possible, and flew the most direct course possible back to Homer. I figured if Homer was fogged in, I would go over to Kenai and fly the ILS to the ground there. At least there would be nothing to hit, and I would not hurt anyone.

Time seemed to drag on interminably, and I was torn between advancing the throttle to get there sooner before it fogged in and the need to continue at best economy cruise. Some readers may know what it's like to watch those fuel gauges sink down toward empty. In the moonlight, I could see a layer of fog covering the entire peninsula. If the engine quit I would have to sink down into the fog with no hope of a good outcome. Finally as I came over the Ptarmigan Hills, there were the lights of Homer in the clear. I've never seen runway lights that looked more beautiful. Upon checking the tanks with a stick, I found very little fuel left. Probably not enough to get to Kenai. I left Homer early the next morning to pick up the fishermen in Anchorage.

An Inch is as Good as a Mile

One morning the dispatcher called me into the office. We had a charter flight to Anchorage to pick up four men that were coming out to one of the lodges on a fishing vacation. They planned to fish the Kenai River for King Salmon. The Kenai River is one of the premier salmon fishing rivers in the world. It is a famous destination for people from many countries, as well as US Citizens.

It was a nice morning, and I enjoyed the flight along the mountains to Anchorage. When I arrived at the gate we shared along with other small commuter airlines, there was only one parking space available right next to the building. I was flying a Cessna 207 that we called the "Bumble Bee" as it was an ugly yellow and black and had not yet been painted in the company colors. I had about 20 minutes to wait until the scheduled departure time, so I went into the terminal to get a cup of coffee. I was half finished with the coffee when I heard airport security paging me. He did not sound happy and seemed to be agitated about something. I immediately went to the gate to see what he wanted.

As soon as I got there and identified myself as the Cook Aviation pilot, he told me in no uncertain terms that I had violated airport regulations and that I was going to be fined. He said if I did not move the airplane immediately our airline would be banned from using the gate. I asked him what regulation I had violated. He said airplanes could not be parked closer than 25 feet from the building. I looked the situation over and made a wild guess. I calmly told him it was not. He got a little red in the face and called on his radio to have another security officer come with a tape measure.

When the officer arrived with the tape measure, they stretched it from the nearest part of the plane to the closest part of the building. They moved it up and down and back and forth. They pulled it so hard I thought it would break, as I was right there closely observing the measurement. The distance was 25 feet and one inch. I could not resist the temptation to act like I knew that all along. From then on, anytime I flew into Anchorage International with a Cook Inlet Aviation plane, I made sure to strictly adhere to all the regulations. The flight back to Homer was more fun than the trip up.

A Knock in the Night

Shortly after I began flying for Cook Inlet Aviation, I was camping in my Volkswagen Van next to the office at the Homer airport while looking for a permanent place to stay. One night about three o'clock in the morning, I was awakened by someone pounding on the van's sliding door. I got my pants on and opened the door. I saw a woman standing there in obvious distress. She was very pregnant and was crying so hard I had a hard time understanding what she was saying. Finally, I understood. She was having contractions and needed to get to the hospital in Anchorage.

She and her husband had made the flight and hospital arrangements with CIA and the Alaska Regional Hospital, but the baby was coming much sooner than expected. Her husband was a fisherman on a large fishing vessel and was out at sea. We had a Cessna 207 out on the line that was ready to go, but I needed to get permission or direction from the airline owner. I tried several times to call him, but apparently he was gone and did not answer.

I called Flight Service to get a weather briefing and found the conditions were favorable. There was a high overcast with good visibility. The woman was getting more and more desperate, as this was her first child. I went out and did a preflight on the plane, making sure it was full of fuel and oil. I took one row of seats out and placed sleeping bags on the floor, in case she needed to lie down. I loaded her into the co-pilots seat and tried to figure out the best way to fasten her seat belt. I taxied out to the runway, checked the magnetos and constant speed propeller, selected the fuel valve, and put down 10 degrees of flaps.

With the landing light illuminating the runway we departed,

climbed up, and set the most direct course for Anchorage. I left the power up fairly high and we made the 123 mile distance in a little less than one hour. 20 miles out, I called Anchorage Approach Control. I explained the situation and requested a flight through their airspace, directly to Merrill Field. I asked Approach to call the hospital and notify them we would arrive in about 12 minutes. I contacted Merrill Tower and got permission to come straight in and land. On short final, my passenger had a bad contraction and I had to yell at her to get her foot off the rudder pedal. There is a taxiway that goes directly to the hospital, and they were waiting for us when we arrived. I felt a wave of relief when they took over.

When I returned to Homer, I was in hot water with Cook Inlet Aviation. I had used the airplane without company authorization. In addition, I had not filed the required flight plan nor arranged for payment from the passenger. Since I had just started flying with CIA, and was unfamiliar with all the regulations, and considering the situation, they let me slide.

After some consideration, it may not have been the most prudent thing to do. I should have taken her to the local clinic and not made the flight to the hospital. However, at that time, I was still new to Homer and did not even know they had a clinic. The woman had her baby about two hours after we arrived at the hospital, and it all worked out for the best.

Chapter II

St. Mary's - Bethel Area

AFTER A LITTLE OVER A YEAR of flying for Cook Inlet Aviation, I went to work for MarkAir Express. At that time MarkAir was the largest commuter airline in Alaska, operating a fleet of DeHavilland Dash 8s, Boeing 737s, and Lockheed Hercules. MarkAir Express operated Cessna 207s, 208s, DeHavilland Twin Otters, and Turbine Beavers. Ordinarily, the shuttle between Bethel and St. Mary's was flown by Twin Otters stationed at Bethel, but sometimes we flew back and forth with C-207s and Cessna Caravans.

My first duty station was at St. Mary's out on the Yukon-Kuskokwim Delta. The YK Delta is named after two large rivers that flow through the area. The Yukon River is 1,980 miles long. It begins in British Columba, Canada and flows through the Canadian territory of the Yukon and Western Alaska before exiting into the Bering Sea. It was the principle means of transport during the Klondike Gold Rush. The Kuskokwim River is 702 miles long and is the longest river in the U.S. that is contained in a single state. It is broad and flat and useful for transportation. The name Kuskokwim comes from the Gwich'in people and means big and slow moving. It also exits into the Bering Sea.

St. Mary's is a hub village with a gravel runway large enough for Boeing 737s and Lockheed C-130s. From St. Mary's we served that whole area, Stebbins, St. Michael, Kotlik, Emmonak, Alakanuk, Sheldon's Point, Scammon Bay, Hooper Bay, Chevak, and Russian Mission and Holy Cross. We also delivered mail and occasional passengers to the Air Force Distant Early Warning radar station out on the Bering seacoast at Cape Romanzof.

The Catholic Church has a mission at St. Mary's and I rented a room there that included kitchen privileges. I had many interesting conversations with the Bishop who also stayed there from time to time. He liked to discuss politics and world affairs, the same things I was interested in. He was a very good pilot, and even in the worst weather, he was on the go with the mission C-206. I guess he figured The Lord would watch over him. The village at St. Mary's is quite a distance from the airport, so I had the company fly out a VW Bug on one of the C-130 trips from Anchorage. I was a popular guy with the other MarkAir pilots stationed there.

The wind was often a problem and I can remember early mornings standing on a ladder fueling the plane when the wind was blowing 20 mph with a temperature around 20 degrees below zero. When I got to feeling sorry for myself, I would think of the pioneers who flew old, open cockpit airplanes without navigation aids or radios. The airplanes of that day were not dependable and there were no airports in the bush for them to land on. Generally, our company rule was that the piston engine airplanes did not fly at temperatures below minus 35 degrees. However, I remember making a life flight trip from Russian Mission to Bethel at night in a C-207 when the temperature was minus 45 degrees. A forced landing in those conditions would be a serious problem.

Spaghetti and Meatballs

One afternoon in the middle of winter, I had a trip to Alakanuk, Emmonak and returned with a load of mail and freight. The weather was right at our company minimums of a 500 foot ceiling and 2 miles visibility. The temperature was 5 degrees below zero with light snow showers, but for once, very little wind. Without the wind, it almost felt warm as I fueled up the Cessna 207. I loaded up nearly 800 pounds of mail which was mostly soda pop that the villagers consumed in large quantities. After checking the weather once more with the village agents, I took off for Alakanuk. I dialed in the LORAN which we used before the GPS system became available. There were white out conditions, but I made it to Alakanuk without a problem.

After unloading the Alakanuk mail, I took off and followed the dark willows on the river the short distance to Emmonak. I had a long wait because our village agent was having problems with the company van. By the time he came, the visibility was getting worse, and it had begun to get dark. I took off for St. Mary's and found I could only keep going by following the willows along the river and watching the heading on the LORAN. I finally got as far as Mountain Village, where the river makes a bend, just short of St. Mary's. The runway elevation at

St. Mary's is 311 feet, about 200 feet above the river. Every time I tried to climb up to land at St. Mary's, I would run into zero visibility. I called the station manager and he reported fog to the ground. I could not get into St. Mary's or Mountain Village, so I had him call Emmonak on the land line to see if I could get in there. The report was that visibility was a little better than when I left, so it was back to following the willows and the LORAN. After landing at Emmonak, I tied the plane down, put on the engine, wing and tail covers, and plugged in the engine heater.

The village agent put me up for the night at his home. The house consisted of three rooms with the curtain across one corner of the main room with a honey bucket. The agent's wife was preparing spaghetti and meatballs for the evening meal, while the agent, his children, and I, were watching TV. She got a chunk of frozen moose burger off the back porch and put it on the counter to thaw out.

While we were watching the TV, I noticed their cat was up on the counter gnawing on the moose burger. When she saw it, she gave it a cuff, knocking it down to the floor. She chopped the burger into chunks and dropped them into a big skillet to cook. The spaghetti was very good and I was glad to get it. The next morning the weather lifted, and I flew the regular schedule. I was glad to return to my clean, warm room at the mission that night too.

Star Light, Star Bright

One night, soon after I began flying for MarkAir Express, I had a flight to Bethel and return. It was wintertime and very cold, but there was very light wind and it seemed almost warm when I fueled up the Cessna 207. The airframe was high time, and a little worn, with fading paint and upholstery, but it had a new engine. We called it the Bethel cruiser because it had a tape deck in the glove compartment that sounded very nice through the headset.

The trip to Bethel was routine, and I had an hour to kill before the scheduled flight back to St. Mary's, so I went up to the restaurant above the terminal to get a burger. I had five passengers going to St. Mary's, and we departed on time. About halfway through the flight, the passengers were all sleeping and I was listening to Merle Haggard singing *Blue Moon* on the tape deck. I could see the stars above, and below, all was dimly white and featureless. Everything was going well and I was enjoying the flight.

Without warning, the entire electrical system failed and nothing worked to get it back. It's a good thing airplane engines are run by magnetos. I reached into my flight bag to get the flashlight I always had there. Unfortunately, someone had borrowed it while the plane was parked at Bethel and I was unable to see the compass or the instruments that were still working. I was worried that I had gotten off course while searching through my flight bag. There were no visible features on the ground, and of course no useable navigation instruments without the electrical system.

I went along for about five minutes wondering what to do, when I remembered a conversation I had previously with one of the other pilots a week earlier. He had mentioned that on the course to St. Mary's he noticed the nose of the airplane was pointing to the third star in the handle of the Big Dipper. I put the nose on it and after about 20 minutes of worry and concern, way out there on the nose was the beacon at St. Mary's. I was reminded of a verse from Bryant's poem "To a Waterfowl."

"There is a Power, whose care
Teaches thy way along that pathless coast,—
The desert and illimitable air,
Lone wandering, but not lost."

When we got to St. Mary's, I had no radio to activate the runway lights but the station manager heard us fly over and keyed the lights with the base station radio in the office. I was able to land without incident, although without benefit of flaps or landing lights. My passengers never realized anything was wrong. They did not wake up till we touched down. Years later, I saw the Bethel cruiser in Anchorage. It had been completely refurbished inside and out and it was beautiful, like new. Unfortunately, the tape deck was gone. From that time until now, if I am flying at night, I make sure to have a working flashlight.

Bethel Blues

One afternoon while I was stationed at St. Mary's, I had a trip to Bethel with four passengers. Although it is only about 85 miles to Bethel from St. Mary's, I filled the tanks of the 207 with the full 80 gallons. I had learned over the years that fuel is your friend when flying the bush. It was the middle of winter and very cold with marginal visibility that deteriorated as we neared Bethel. When I dialed in the ATIS, it was reporting one mile visibility.

Bethel is a large hub airport that serves many small villages in the region, and there were several small Part 135 airlines operating out of Bethel. MarkAir and Alaska Airlines each had two flights a day with Boeing Jets. There was always a lot of traffic, and since the visibility was down to one mile, all the small airline planes had to request a special VFR clearance into the control zone. I was fifth in line, so I had to wait my turn. We all entered holding patterns waiting for our turn. Two large jets came in on IFR clearances, so the holding time for our plane was an hour and forty-five minutes. Finally, everybody got safely on the ground, but the weather was below the MarkAir Express Company minimums, so I was stuck in Bethel for the night.

The Company owned a house in Bethel where the local MarkAir Express pilots stayed. At any one time, there were four to six guys living there, and it was the typical bachelor dive one might expect. Dirty clothes were piled around, dishes in the sink, and fruit flies filled the air. Water was in short supply so it was necessary to use as little as possible.

The wind picked up and it began to snow a regular blizzard. I had the plane tied down with engine, wing, and tail covers. The engine heater was plugged in so the plane was set for the night. When it was time to go to the pilot house, it was dark and very cold. The company had a four wheel drive Chevrolet Suburban for the pilots to use. When we got to the house, the road grader had plowed a big berm of ice and snow across the driveway. We had to get out and shovel the snow berm to get into the driveway. In the morning it was still snowing and the road grader had already done his thing again. We had to go out in the wind and 20 degrees below zero temperature and shovel out the driveway in order to drive to the terminal. The weather stayed down all day with high winds and heavy snow, so it was another night on the floor of the pilot house. When we got there, the grader had once again done the deed and we had to shovel the driveway again.

Just as we came in the door, the phone rang. The call was for the Twin Otter pilot. It was from Hawaii, and they wanted him to come over and fly Twin Otters in Hawaii for more money. The next day the weather cleared, and I was able to get back to St. Mary's that night to stay in my nice clean, warm room.

LIFE FLIGHT TO BETHEL

Late one afternoon, we were hanging around the terminal at St. Mary's after the day's schedule had been run. It was mid-summer, and daylight lasted almost 24 hours a day. The nurse from the clinic came in with a mother and her eight year old daughter. The girl was suffering terrible abdominal pain, and sweating profusely. The pain was centered in the lower right quadrant of her abdomen.

I had served in the medical corps as a surgical tech and had scrubbed in on several appendectomies. It seemed obvious to me, and also to the nurse, that appendicitis was the problem. The nurse was talking to the Alaska Native Medical Center in Anchorage, trying to get authorization for a charter flight to Bethel. This went on for almost an hour with no apparent progress. The child's pain suddenly abated, and she was lying quietly, but still with a high fever. I suspected that her appendix had ruptured and that she needed to get to the hospital in Bethel immediately. The nurse was in agreement. I told the station manager that I would pay for the charter and that we would be leaving immediately.

The plane was full of fuel and I just needed to remove one row of seats to put the stretcher in. I loaded up the girl, her mother, and the nurse, and told the dispatcher to notify Bethel of our estimated time of arrival and to have an ambulance at the terminal. I already knew the weather was flyable, with very little wind for a change. After I gave an expedited briefing and runup, we departed and I kept the power up all the way. When we arrived at Bethel, I called the tower and requested priority for a life flight. The ambulance was there and the young girl, her mother, and the nurse were on their way to the hospital. The girl did indeed have a ruptured appendix, and the doctor said it would have been very dangerous to have waited any longer. He was angry that the authorization for the flight had not been made immediately.

When the Native Health Service found out that it really was an emergency, they authorized payment for the charter. I came out feeling relieved that I had been able to help the girl. It's amazing to me that the bureaucrats were more concerned with the paperwork than the life of a young child. The doctor said he was going to see to it that things would be changed.

The girl made a full recovery and I often saw her at the village store. She was a cute little thing and always had a big smile for me.

Chapter III

Cold Bay

After I had been flying at St. Mary's, Alaska for nearly a year, the chief pilot came through looking for someone to station at Cold Bay, Alaska. Cold Bay is located near the tip of the Alaska Peninsula, where the Aleutian Chain of islands begins. It was a one man and a one airplane show, with company-supplied living quarters across the road from the airport.

The airplane would be a Cessna 208 Caravan, which was good, but the weather there was notoriously bad. Cold Bay sits at the boundary where the weather patterns from the Pacific Ocean and the Bering Sea collide. This results in high winds, thick heavy clouds, rain, snow, and fog. Cold Bay is the cloudiest, windiest place in the United States. I told him I would take it. A one man operation appealed to me.

There is one thing constant about the weather at the tip of the Alaskan Peninsula, and that is you can never be sure what it is going to do. After flying for several years and thousands of hours at Cold Bay, one thing stands out. Fuel is your friend. I never left on a flight without taking on as much fuel as I could, considering the load and runway conditions where I would be landing. This practice saved my bacon on more than one occasion.

The Cold Bay Airport is large, more than 10,000 feet long and 150 feet wide. It has good instrument approaches and good lighting. If the weather turned bad, I could climb up, go on instruments, and make an ILS approach into Cold Bay. The years I flew at Cold Bay were before we had the GPS system. There were no moving maps, no artificial vision, and no terrain warnings. I had to know exactly where I was at all times. I had a LORAN, ADF, and a DME, which would give a course and distance, but nothing about the terrain in between.

The Cessna Caravan is a wonderful airplane for the type of loads and conditions I faced while flying the bush in Alaska. The company had the Caravan outfitted with aluminum checker plate floors and mud flaps on the main gear. I hauled barrels of gas, lumber, explosives, four wheelers, and about anything else you can think of. Sometimes the planes came back covered in mud, like a four wheel drive pickup. I landed on beaches, sand bars, tide flats, sand blows in the tundra, and many narrow sand and dirt airstrips. I landed with full loads onto landing strips as short as 900 feet.

Much of the time flights were conducted in high winds, rain, fog, and snow. Many of the routes on the Pacific side of the peninsula were along steep rocky shorelines that slanted off into deep water. It was a good feeling to be flying behind a Pratt and Whitney PT6 turbine engine that was smooth, powerful, and bullet proof. The Caravans I flew in Alaska never let me down, and none of the thousands of passengers I carried ever got a scratch.

Ice Over Belkofski Bay

One day in January, 1991, while I was based at Cold Bay, Alaska, I was making my first scheduled flight of the day from Cold Bay to King Cove. From there my flight would continue north, up the coast to Sand Point, located in the Shumagin Islands, and return. The Cessna Caravan assigned to me had anti-ice boots on the wings and stabilizers, a hot plate on the windshield, and heated prop and pitot. That plane had gone to King Salmon for a one hundred hour inspection, and they sent one down for the day that had no anti-ice equipment except for a heated pitot; because it was used on floats during the summer.

King Cove Airport facing Belkofski Bay

The weather was cold, in the mid-20 degrees Fahrenheit, with a high overcast, no precipitation in the forecast and no visible moisture. A strong wind was coming from the Pacific side of the peninsula, so it was a rough ride going through the pass to King Cove. I dropped off the mail and picked up two fishermen going to Sand Point. Ordinarily, I turned left through a narrow pass between Mt. Belkofski and Mt. Pavlov toward Volcano Bay. But I had learned the hard way not to do that when there was a strong wind coming from the Pacific Ocean over Mt. Belkofski. Instead, I planned to climb straight out past Mt. Belkofski before turning up the coast toward Sand Point.

We had gone about two miles and climbed to 2,500 feet when it started raining large drops that froze on the plane immediately. Despite full bleed-air defrost, the windshield was completely covered with ice in about a minute. I thought about trying to climb to warmer air, but gave that up when I saw the wings already had ice on the leading edge and it was building rapidly. The Caravan has a poor reputation in icing conditions, and I knew we had to get back on the ground immediately.

The company manual for the Caravan said no more than 20 degrees of flaps, and no slower than 95 knots when carrying ice. I made a carefully coordinated 270 degree turn to the right, away from the mountain so that when we came around I would be able to see the airstrip out the left. We were way high, with a 25 mile per hour tailwind, but the sink rate was so great it looked like it would work. By now the wings had built up over an inch of ice on the leading edges and the prop was beginning to vibrate. When I was lined up with the runway, I turned toward it and held that heading.

The King Cove airport lies in a narrow valley with mountains all around. It is marked hazardous on the chart for good reason. When the winds are strong there, dangerous turbulence and wind shear is present. Since 1980, eleven people have been killed landing or taking off at King Cove. Any attempt to fly the pattern and land into the wind would end in disaster. There are large boulders and rock ledges on both sides and the approach, so we had to hit the airstrip or we would not survive the crash.

The elevators began to pulse and I knew the stabilizers were about ready to stall. If that happened, we would dive straight into the ground. We continued down and when the end of the runway flashed by, we were 30 feet high and 20 feet to the right of center. I had just enough time to correct to the left before we were down. When I went to flare, there was no flare and we banged down hard. We had used up 1,200 feet. I flipped the flaps up and applied all the brakes I could get, while pulling the prop into full reverse as hard as it would go. The torque almost pulled us off the runway, but I managed to save it right on the edge. I held that all the way to the end of the 3,500 foot strip and had just enough room to turn around and taxi back to the ramp. I had to have the fisherman in the right seat call my turn onto the ramp. The two guys were laughing and thought it was really cool. I could hardly pry my hands off the controls. Just imagine driving your car down a narrow gravel road at a 130 miles an hour with the windshield covered!

I stayed on the runway by looking directly out the left. The strange thing is, that I was so concentrated on what I was doing, I was never afraid until we stopped. When I got out, the ice measured one and one-half inches on the leading edges of the wings. The struts and landing gear legs were the same. The stabilizers had fingers of ice on the leading edges that looked like a comb. The prop spinner had a big mound of ice and the prop blades were coated with ice. We were just fortunate that the high rate of descent was exactly what we needed. It would have been impossible to maintain level flight.

I decided I was done for the rest of the day. I notified the company, tied the Caravan down and went home with our village agent. We came back the next day with scrapers, ladders, and de-ice fluid, and it took two hours to clean off the ice. I was thankful to get my regular Caravan back the following day. I let the company know I would not fly any plane at Cold Bay in the winter unless it had anti-ice equipment.

Murphy's Law (If It Can Go Wrong . . .)

For three and a half years I was stationed near the tip of the Alaska Peninsula at Cold Bay. Cold Bay is the cloudiest, and tied with St. Paul Island, Alaska, as the windiest place in the United States. It always amazes me how things can go from completely normal to gunnysack in a matter of seconds. I was making the scheduled morning flight from Cold Bay to King Cove. It is a short flight across the bay to Leonard Harbor and then through the pass to the King Cove airstrip.

When the wind is blowing hard, you go through the pass on one side or the other to avoid the wind shear and turbulence which is almost always there. The mountains rise steeply on each side and it can get very rough. It was one of those days that no matter which side I chose it was borderline severe. Pencils on the instrument panel were flying up and down the windshield, and I could hardly keep my feet on the rudder pedals. Again, the King Cove airport is marked hazardous on the chart for good reason.

I had a pretty good load of mail and canned goods in the belly pod, along with six passengers in the cabin. They were hanging onto their seats and not saying a word. A young fellow was sitting in the co-pilots seat and I had given him strict instructions to not touch anything. Just as we were coming to some small hills in the narrowest part of the pass that we called the camel humps, he inexplicably put his hand close to the red fuel condition lever and asked "what does that do?" Just then we hit a smasher and his hand knocked the lever into idle cutoff. The engine quit instantly.

The Caravan can be restarted without going through the whole routine, if you catch it before it goes below 50% RPM. I immediately slapped the fuel back on and swept the switches on the left panel, the starter, ignition, and fuel pump. I set the throttle and looked for a place to set down. I feathered the prop, so I could glide to a small sand bar in Delta Creek that I knew about. I heard a relight on the engine, but it takes a while to spool up, and even then, the prop had gone to feather and it had to come into pitch.

We were down to about 50 feet and a forced landing was imminent. I lined up on the small sand bar in the creek, and was reaching for the flaps, when the power came back with a tremendous surge because I firewalled the throttle. We climbed back up and finished going through the pass and landed, happy to be down in one piece, but mad at the guy who had nearly crashed us.

The other passengers were mad at him also, and he walked over to the side of the ramp looking very dejected. After I cooled down, I went over and apologized, and told him I was sorry I had yelled at him. I told him that I realized what had happened was unintentional, and nothing would be done about it. I told him he could ride with me any time he wanted, and he did many times while I was based at Cold Bay. I always let him ride in the front, because I knew he would never cause a problem again. From that time until now, I have always instructed passengers not to put their hands close to any controls, unless I know what they are doing. I make sure they know I am serious and not just mouthing the words.

Flight Service Reporting: Weather way below legal minimums. Civil twilight, fog to the water, half mile visibility, strong wind over the flanks of Mt Dutton. There will be dangerous wind shear, turbulence, and a quartering 20 knot tailwind going through Delta Creek pass.

POEM: LIFE FLIGHT TO KING COVE

Flying out low across Cold Bay,
white caps dimly visible in the gloom.
Ten degrees of flap and throttled back,
the shoreline's coming up soon.

I search ahead and out the left,
through a windshield rain streaked and dirty.
Suddenly, there, right off the wing,
the rocks at a hundred and thirty.

With two lives to save, or three to lose,
every nerve is tense at attention
as shadowy shapes in shades of gray
loom out like an apparition.

King Cove Airport facing Delta Creek Pass

More sensed than seen they guide me along,
into the head of the bay.
There's no turning back, I'm committed
to go in the rest of the way.

As I round the point, the wind shear strikes.
The Caravan drops and shudders.
My flight bag sails up between the seats
and my feet won't stay on the rudders.

My mouth is dry, my legs are shaking,
my hearts beating way too fast.
Lord, put your hands on mine, or
this flight could be my last.

Ten minutes of this, an eternity more,
there's Delta Creek. I have to keep it in sight.
I've got to get past the Camel Humps,
somewhere close by on the right.

As I edge on around, there's the road,
and there's the bonfire flame.
All that's left is to land, strap them in,
and go back the way I came.

False Pass Fiasco

It began as a routine mail run to False Pass. False Pass is situated near the tip of the Alaska Peninsula, where the chain of Aleutian Islands begins. The wind blowing from the south at 30 knots is common out there. This particular day, visibility was also marginal with snow squalls passing through the area. I headed out over Applegate Cove and turned south down the Bering Sea coast, to the entrance of Bechavin Bay and the False Pass Channel. I had learned the hard way that when a strong wind is coming from the south, the best way to get to the False Pass Village is to fly close to the mountains in the lee of the wind to escape the turbulence. I made it to False Pass without a problem, although the windsock at each end of the airstrip was standing straight out, pointing toward the center. A reversible prop is a good thing.

Fortunately, there were no passengers wanting to go to Cold Bay. When I looked down the channel I noticed that snow squalls had spread out and were blocking the channel in both directions. There was blue sky directly overhead, so I decided to climb up and go over the top and deal with the turbulence. I climbed up over the snow squalls to about 2,500 feet and headed down the channel.

Suddenly, the plane was hit by a hard jolt that yanked me up from my seat. I was shocked to see that my seatbelt was coming loose. Before I could do anything it happened again, and I flew up and hit my head on the windshield frame. I remember thinking how strange the instrument panel looked from that angle. The third time it happened was the worst, and I was momentarily stunned.

False Pass Airport

When I regained my senses, I was flying along a shoreline in heavy snow and very limited visibility. I could fly the airplane without difficulty, but blood was running down my face. I could not remember where I was or where I was going. I wiped the blood off my face with a towel I always carried in my flight bag and continued that way for several minutes, just trying to follow the shoreline. Finally, I came to the opening where the False Pass Channel reached the Bering Sea coast. There is a formation there called Cape Krenitzen that has a distinctive hooked shape. The moment I saw it, my situational awareness snapped back into place.

I turned to the heading for Cold Bay and made it there without difficulty. After landing at Cold Bay, I examined the seatbelt and found that it was defective. I had a bad cut, a big lump on my head, and two chipped teeth. I examined the windshield frame very carefully, and could find no damage. I got a ladder and looked at the top of the wings, expecting to see some wrinkles or popped rivets. All was normal, and I came to the conclusion the Caravan was a lot tougher than I was.

Looking back on it, I do not fault my decision to fly over the top of the snow squall. If the seatbelt had not come loose, I would probably remember it only as a rough ride. I finished my third week on duty, and then went to Anchorage for my week off. After my time off, and a trip to the dentist, I was good as new and ready to go again.

From that time until now, every time I fly a different airplane I always carefully examine the seatbelts to make sure they are installed and operate correctly. I believe that is a good thing to do for anyone flying a new or unfamiliar plane.

Life Flight from Port Moller

In January, 1991, I finished my schedule for the day at Cold Bay, Alaska. It had been a busy one with two extra flights to the small 900 foot gravel strip at Herendeen Bay. I was hauling provisions to the Blue Wave Company's fish processing ship, Alaska Coastal Star, anchored there. I could land there with a 2,500 pound load but had to takeoff empty without a lot of fuel due to soft runway conditions. I had been dealing with wind, fog, and rain all day and was tired and looking forward to supper.

When I got back to Cold Bay, I fueled up the Caravan and had just pulled into my tie downs, when the station manager came out and told me we had a charter to Port Moller, then Sand Point, and return. I knew a big storm was coming, but after checking with Flight Service, I figured I could do the charter and get back before it arrived. I had one passenger going to Port Moller, and we made the 87 miles up the Bering Sea coast in good time. After dropping him off, I loaded up two going to Sand Point, located in the Shumagin Island group over the mountains on the Pacific side of the Alaska Peninsula. I was just advancing the throttle for takeoff when I saw the old cannery Suburban bouncing along the road flashing his headlights. I shut down and waited for him to drive down the runway.

I was very concerned when I heard the message. A crewman on the crab fishing boat, Barbarossa, had been seriously injured by a falling 400 pound crab pot. The boat was heading for Port Moller and they needed me to wait and take the injured man to Cold Bay. A life flight jet would be coming there to take the man to the hospital in Anchorage. It was going to take the Barbarossa at least three hours to make it to Port Moller and the storm would have arrived. I agreed to wait, although I knew it would be dark and there would be a very strong crosswind. I taxied back to the ramp and my passengers rode back to the bunkhouse for the night. The wind was already picking up as I tied the Caravan down to some heavy stacks of road grader blades. For some reason the cannery guy left without giving me a ride, and I had to walk the half mile back past the garbage dump. I was glad the bears that usually hung out there were probably denned up for the winter.

I waited in the old cannery warehouse for the 98 foot steel crab fishing vessel, Barbarossa, to arrive. Three hours later, the wind was rattling the metal roof so loudly I thought it was going to blow off, and snow was falling heavily. The Barbarossa finally arrived, and I was amazed the captain could make it with the wind and snowstorm in the dark. We loaded the injured man into the Suburban and headed out to the plane. Snow was already drifting over the ruts that passed as a road. We loaded him into the plane and strapped him down. I got my flashlight and looked at the wings. Much to my relief the wind was blowing the snow off and they were clean. I ran down the runway to check for drifts. Fortunately, there were only three small ones about six inches deep with soft snow which would not be a problem. When I got back to the plane, I secured the rudder lock and loosed the tie downs. I climbed up into the cockpit and got the engine started.

I was parked 90 degrees to the runway, and when I got the panel lights on, the airspeed indicator was showing 40 knots and the Caravan was dancing and rocking in the wind. The crosswind was going to be a serious problem. When I turned on the landing lights, I was almost blinded by the dazzling whiteness of the snow. I taxied out, turned to the runway heading, and went through the check list twice just to be sure. On each side, I could see two red cones plainly and a third one most of the time, which meant the runway visual range was 600 feet. There was a very strong illusion that the cones and the Caravan were moving sideways at 40 knots, and the rest of the world was standing still. The wind was from the left, so I got over to the right side of the runway as far as I could and aimed for the third cone on the left.

I put down 20 degrees of flaps, and with full aileron into the wind, firewalled the throttle right past the torque limit line as hard as it would go. The Caravan surged ahead, and we crabbed down the runway toward the third cone. Just as we were coming up on it, the plane started slipping and sliding to the right. When we were about to go off, I put down full flaps and the good old Caravan began to fly. There were no obstructions on the left, so I let it turn into the wind. My only thoughts were 'wings level, positive rate of climb, and airspeed.' I set the flaps and pulled the power back before the temps got too high.

We bounced and jolted our way up through the maelstrom and broke into the clear at 3000 feet, to the most fantastic array of stars and planets I have ever seen. The sky was lit up from horizon to horizon. We did not have GPS back then, so with the LORAN and the ADF pointing the way to Cold Bay, I had time to think about the thousands, maybe millions, of years the light had been streaming toward the Earth. I thought of the moment in time we have to live. I thought about the man in back and how uncertain life really is. I got to wondering if there are other planets like ours, where men fish for crabs in the wintertime.

When we got to Cold Bay, I called to see where the life flight jet was and then made a DME arc to the Localizer and down the ILS. When I finally saw the approach lights, I was surprised they were over on the left because of the very strong crosswind. I finally got the right wheel to touch, came back on the prop, and we were down. I taxied over to the small clinic and we made the injured man as comfortable as possible. The life flight jet arrived in a few minutes, and the man was soon on his way to Anchorage where he recovered from his injuries.

Postscript

A few weeks later, on February 10, the Barbarossa left St. George Island at eleven o'clock at night to go out to the fishing grounds. Two hours later three boats in the area heard a distress call saying "I am going over." The call was attributed to the Barbarossa. No trace of the Barbarossa, or any of its six man crew, has ever been found.

Barbarossa (1989)

Motor Man

One morning, just before the opening of the salmon fishing season, we got a call from a fisherman at Port Moller. His boat engine had blown up, and he had a new one shipped out to Cold Bay on a Northern Air Cargo DC-6. Sometimes the salmon fishing season is only open for a few days, so he was desperate to get it and have his boat ready to go. If he missed the season opening, it would cost him many thousands of dollars.

He had checked with our company in Anchorage and they had

told him it would fit in the Cessna Caravan. It was a big Caterpillar Diesel that weighed over 2900 pounds. The Caravan has a large cargo door on the left side, at the back of the cabin. I measured the engine and determined that it would just fit in the door if two of the accessories were removed and the crate it came in was taken off. I didn't want to haul it, because I knew it would be hard on the airplane. The Caravan would carry the weight, but it should be more evenly distributed and not concentrated in one area.

The company insisted that we haul it, because they had promised him that we would, and they wanted our airline to be considered a can-do outfit by the locals. The airplane sits at a tail low attitude when resting on the tail stand. When we eased the engine through the door and let it down, one of the forks on the forklift would not come out without pulling the airplane sideways. If that happened with all that weight at the back it would be a disaster.

We raised the engine back up and put some blocks under the tail stand so the plane would sit level with the weight on it. I blocked the main gear and tied the tail to a ramp tug and a pickup so it could not swing sideways. I had placed some small lengths of 3/4 inch pipe under the pallet, so I could use a come along to pull the engine forward. It had to move right up close to the pilot's seat so the weight and balance would be correct. While we were moving the engine forward I could hear the fuselage flexing, a terrible way to treat a million dollar airplane. Finally, when I had it jacked forward into position, I tied it with straps every way possible, but I knew I would be smashed like a bug in any off airport landing.

The weather at Cold Bay was marginal, but the fellow who owned the engine said the weather at Port Moller was "real good." It has been my experience over the years that the weather reports from the villages often depend more on how badly they want something than the actual weather. I made my way the 87 miles up the Bering Sea coast. Passing Nelson Lagoon, I could see a layer of fog covering Port Moller that extended almost to the head of the bay.

I flew up to the head of the bay and was able to duck under the fog layer and follow the shore line back to the cannery. As I flew along, the visibility grew steadily worse, and soon it got to the point I could barely make it out. The cannery came up before I expected it and by the time I saw it, it was too late to turn and follow the road to the airport. I had to climb up through the fog layer and do the whole thing over again.

On the next attempt, I was able to make the turn in time to follow the road out to the airport and land. The man who owned the boat motor didn't have the nerve to come out to the airport, because he knew I would be mad. He sent two of his crewmen with a little forklift that had small rubber tires made for hard surfaces. The thing would hardly move on the soft gravel of the ramp. I couldn't fault him for that though, because equipment is hard to come by out in the bush. I chocked the main gear, blocked the tail stand, and then tied the tail so it couldn't move sideways.

I got the boat engine moved back to the cargo door with the come-along. We had a heck of a time getting the forklift moved up into position. After about a half hour of messing around, and a little yelling here and there, we finally had it moved up into position to raise the engine. I had my doubts, but with a lot of creaking and smoke from its engine, the little forklift finally lifted it into the air. The next problem was to get it away from the airplane. The forklift could not move on the soft gravel, so we chained it to their old pickup.

The pickup needed a clutch, so it would not pull without jerking. With the weight up high and the instability caused by the soft ground, I was scared to death it would fall against the door frame or the stabilizer. When it was back far enough, we let it down and pulled it away from the plane. When you think about it, the little bit we got for the freight, was not worth the strain on the airplane and the chance of serious damage. Finding the airport in the fog, with a 3,000 pound motor behind my back is something I will never do again.

When the fishing season was over, I noticed that the fisherman who had ordered the motor sent his crew out on PenAir.

Bear Tales

Bear at the Window
Late one afternoon, the Flight Service Station at Cold Bay warned us that a very powerful storm was due to arrive overnight. I had finished my schedule for the day, so I tied the Caravan down, facing the direction of the wind. The anchors were set in concrete, and I used double straps. I installed gust locks on the controls and had a floodlight illuminating it, so it could be observed during the night.

In the early morning hours, I was awakened to a tremendous sound from the wind, and my quarters being shaken. I got up and looked at the anemometer, and it was showing 75 miles per hour with stronger gusts every few minutes. I went into the kitchen where there was a large window to see the Caravan across the road. I had my face pressed against the window, intently watching to see how the plane was withstanding the storm. All was stable and it appeared to be handling the wind quite well.

I noticed a movement out of the corner of my eye, and when I turned to look, there was a huge brown bear standing just outside looking at me with his face about two feet from mine. I saw the wind blowing his fur and the rain running down his face. His ears looked about as wide apart as my shoulders. It was a real shocker. I backed away quickly and moved around the corner out of sight. He did not appear aggressive, just curious.

Shopping for Groceries
One of our ticket agents at Cold Bay had an experience that was kind of scary, but funny at the same time. She and her husband, who worked at Flight Service, had a small home at Cold Bay near the airport. They had placed several piles of top soil around the house; intending to plant a lawn during the summer.

In winter, the days are short and it gets dark early. She had gone to the store to buy groceries and their parking spot was some distance from the house. Upon her return, she made several trips carrying groceries and walked right past what she thought was a pile of dirt. The next morning, the pile of dirt was gone, and she realized it wasn't a pile of dirt but actually a large bear.

The Whale at Navy town

During trips to King Cove from Cold Bay, the PenAir pilots and I had noticed a dead whale washed up on the beach near what we called Navy Town. There were remnants of what used to be foundations of a good sized group of buildings that were laid during WWII. The place where the whale washed up was below a steep bank, almost a cliff, about 75 feet high. After a few days there were five large brown bears eating on it.

There was a road that went from the airport to a place where it was possible to look down at the bears. Some of the Reeve Aleutian ground crew heard about it. They decided they would drive out there and have a look. When they got there, they parked about 50 feet from the edge and looked over to observe the bears. They had no more than poked their heads over when they were spotted by a huge male bear. He came charging right up the steep bank and they ran for their lives. They jumped into the car and closed the doors just in time. It is amazing how fast those bears can move when they want to.

Fishing for Silvers

There is a very nice small stream that flows into Cold Bay near the airport. When the silver salmon are running, the fishing is outstanding. One day, when the silver salmon run was at its peak, one of the PenAir pilots and I decided to go down to the river to do some fishing. The river had some sandbars that one could walk out on to cast their lures. There are also some areas of thick brush and some open spaces. We were catching Silvers on almost every cast and releasing them all. Soon, it just became work. We stopped fishing and were standing on the sandbar talking about flying in the Cold Bay area.

It was a nice sunny day, which was quite rare out there. We were suddenly surprised and a little frightened when a huge male bear got up from where he had been laying in the brush. We had no idea that he was there, only about 50 feet from where we were standing. He looked at us curiously, without aggression. We did not look directly at him, as that could be a sign of aggression. He knew we were there from the time we walked out on the sandbar. He started moving and waded over to our side of the river. When he got to our side, he stood and looked at us for a moment, and then he walked away. He was a fine specimen in his prime, and I wished that I had a camera.

Bear at the Footbridge

One day, during the bear watching season at Brooks Lake, we flew some tourists out to observe the bears. One of the passengers was an elderly woman who had lagged behind the others. She was walking down the path and came to a footbridge that crossed a small creek. She was about halfway over the bridge when she saw a bear charging straight at her. It ran by so closely that it brushed against her. It was actually going for a bear on the other side of the bridge. She demanded to be taken back to the plane and would not get out until we were back in King Salmon.

Adrenaline Rush

One evening after business hours at the only restaurant in Cold Bay, two ladies came to do the cleaning, which they did every evening. It was in the summertime so it stayed light until late. At that time of year, brown bears were often seen walking around town. The residents had to be aware that one could always be around. After the women had finished cleaning the restaurant, they came out to get in their car. One of the people from Flight Service happened to be watching and saw the whole thing.

The woman driving was coming around to get in the driver's door while the other walked straight out to get in the passenger door. As they were about to get in, they saw a large brown bear running toward them, and it was close. The woman who was about to get in the passenger side door ran back into the restaurant. The woman on the driver's side was quite large, possibly 250 pounds, and she leapt right over the hood of the car and got into the passenger's side. It would be impossible for her to accomplish that under normal circumstances. The bear was not interested in them at all. He was going after another bear some distance away. It is amazing what one can do when the adrenaline hits.

Surprise at the Hangar Door

One morning, in preparation for the day's schedule, I was doing my normal preflight check. I walked over and pressed the button to raise up the hangar door. I was holding the button as the door started up, turning to talk to the mechanic who had replaced the battery overnight. When I turned back to face the door, it had raised about two feet and I saw two sets of huge claws. A large bear was standing right outside the door. I pushed the down button to lower the door as fast as I could. We went to the window and saw the bear shuffling off towards the PenAir hangar, which was open. The bear walked right into their hangar. We got on the phone and alerted them about their visitor. I don't know what they did, but it soon came running out. Another day, another bear encounter in Cold Bay.

Juneau Lake

My brother Bill, and I owned a little Taylorcraft airplane on floats that we kept at Campbell Lake in Anchorage. One weekend, on my time off, my wife and I made plans to fly to Juneau Lake on the Resurrection Trail to camp.

Resurrection Trail is a forest service maintained trail 38 miles long between Hope and Cooper Landing, Alaska. It runs along a valley next to the Chugach Mountains, and Juneau Lake is near its center. Juneau Lake is a beautiful, pristine lake that is visited by many hikers during the summer months. The forest service built a very nice cabin on its shore that can accommodate eight hikers.

The weather was perfect with clear, blue skies and very little wind. When we arrived at the lake, the surface was dead calm, so we had to make a glassy water landing. A glassy water landing is actually a fun thing to do. When you are close to touchdown, it is impossible to tell exactly how high you are because you have no depth perception. You have to set up a correct rate of decent and hold that until you touchdown.

We beached the airplane and unloaded our gear. For a change, there were very few mosquitos. While we were circling to land, we noticed a nice small stream a short distance up the trail and decided to go and get a jug of fresh water there. The trail was good except for a few spots that were wet and muddy with some fairly sharp bends and high brush on each side. We had gone about 100 yards, and as we walked around a bend, we saw a set of the largest bear tracks I had ever seen. They were fresh tracks, and the water on the trail was still running into them.

That bear was very near. We did not have any firearms or bear spray. It was enough to make the hair on your neck stand up. The tracks were going away from us, so he must have known we were there. We began to talk loudly and even sang to make sure he was aware of us. We continued on a few more steps to get our water. I was very happy to leave the area and get back to camp.

That evening was a magical time. The summer days were long and it stayed light almost all night long. A big moose came out of the woods and waded out into the lake. He swam over to the other side. It was a sight to behold to see that big rack of horns going across the lake. That, along with the moonlight, and the cry of a loon, was an experience I will never forget.

The Perryville Pee-In

The Alaska State Police chartered the Caravan for a trip to Perryville where there had been a suspicious death that needed to be investigated. Perryville is a small village located on the Pacific side of the Alaska Peninsula, between Sand Point and the Chignik's. To get there from Sand Point, you have to wind your way back along an irregular shoreline. As usual, the weather was marginal with fog and wind. We were able to fly there using the LORAN and RADAR, despite very poor visibility.

The state trooper was a lady who was about thirty five years old. She was not very big, but her size was more than made up for with courage and determination. She was very nice but all business. The airport at Perryville is located around a bend about a mile from the village. Considering the situation, I asked her if she wanted me to go with her. She said, "No, wait at the plane." I watched her disappear around the bend walking tall. About an hour and a half went by and I was beginning to be concerned. A few minutes more, however, and here she came, marching five men ahead of her. As they drew near, I could see that the men were all drunk. I don't know what she said to them at the village, but none of them seemed inclined to cause any trouble.

I let down the air stair door and loaded them up. They were too drunk to figure out their seatbelts, so I made sure they were all buckled in correctly. The Trooper sat behind them where she could keep an eye on them. I got into my seat and fastened my seat belt. Just as I turned on the fuel pump to start the engine, one of the worthies yelled out, "I have to pee." I got out of my seat, unbuckled the complainer, and took him outside.

When he was finished we got back in and went through the seat belt drill again. Just as I turned the fuel pump on again, one of the others yelled out, "I have to pee." I looked at the trooper and she looked at me. We took them all outside, lined them up and told them "It's now or never." After they had done the deed, I loaded them up and strapped them in. Considering their inebriated condition, I was glad the trip to Sand Point was uneventful. I waited at Sand Point for the van to transport them to jail, and then made my way to Cold Bay for the afternoon schedule. It was all in a day's work for the trooper.

Stuck Again in Cold Bay

The last year I was stationed out at Cold Bay, the company began flying DeHavilland Dash 8s out to Dutch Harbor with a stop at Cold Bay. One Monday morning, the flight made the stop at Cold Bay and then went on to Dutch Harbor. Because of the weather, they were unable to land. They held in the area for quite a while, hoping visibility would improve, but finally had to give it up and return to Cold Bay for fuel.

I was out making my last run of the day to Nelson Lagoon, Port Moller, and Sand Point. When I got back to Cold Bay, I was surprised to see the Dash 8 still sitting on the ramp. After I parked and tied down the Caravan for the night, I went into the office and found out they had been unable to fuel because something was wrong with the underwing fuel port. They were unable to get fuel to flow into the wing tanks.

I told the Dash 8 captain that I might be able to fuel the plane from up on top of the wings. I had the ramp crew lift me up with the Caterpillar 988 Loader. I fueled the plane up through the fuel ports on the top of the wings. Meanwhile, the company made the decision to have the Dash 8 stay overnight at Cold Bay and try for Dutch Harbor in the morning. There were only a few passengers on board, and the company put them up at the small motel at Cold Bay.

Later that evening, Flight Service notified us that a big storm was coming in with winds up to 75 miles per hour. We chained down the Dash 8 and parked the big Caterpiller front loader near it to block some of the wind.

The next morning, the wind was still blowing hard with powerful gusts every few minutes. I had the Caravan tied down with double straps facing into the wind, so it was in no danger. The Dash 8 crew had gone to breakfast at the restaurant. After they finished eating, I saw them making their way up the road toward the office. They were leaning into the wind, and having a difficult time of it. Two or three minutes later, I felt a huge gust of wind shake my quarters. I looked out the window just in time to see a large section of the roof blow off the restaurant and land on the road where the crew had been walking. It probably would have killed them all.

The Dash 8 never did get to Dutch Harbor, and the crew took it back to Anchorage later that day. I remained grounded for three days because of the storm. Due to the roof damage, we couldn't eat in the restaurant for quite a while. Instead, the remaining passengers, PenAir crew, and I went down to the Weathered Inn, the local bar built by the Flying Tigers after World War II.

The passengers finally made it to Dutch Harbor on another flight later that week, but the weather made me think back to the Second World War, when the young 23 year olds flying P-38s and P-40s lived in tents in very primitive conditions. They flew the Aleutian chain in some of the worst weather conditions on earth, with none of the modern navigation equipment that we enjoy today. The Japanese bombed Dutch Harbor and invaded some of the other Aleutian Islands. The Aleutian campaign fought there turned the war in favor of the United States. My hat's off to them.

Unscheduled Landing

My afternoon scheduled flight was full, with all seats occupied. The fellow sitting in the
co-pilot's seat was a young man who seemed like a normal, average passenger. I gave my usual briefing and instructed him not to touch anything. We left Cold Bay and headed up the Bering Sea

Coast, with planned stops at Nelson Lagoon and Port Moller. The weather was good for a change, and I was enjoying the calm wind and visibility.

We had gone about 40 miles up the Bering Sea coast and were near Black Hill. I was looking out the side window at some caribou as we cruised along. Suddenly, without any warning, the Caravan made a violent, steep bank and diving turn to the right. Shocked, I forced the control back to level flight and had to use a lot of pressure to maintain control. I immediately saw the cause. The fellow in the right seat was wrestling me for the controls and I yelled at him to let go. He acted like he did not hear or understand what I was saying. It was all I could do to overpower him and keep control of the airplane. The man who was seated directly behind him loosened his seat belt so he could move forward. He got the guy in choke hold and pulled him backward, into his seat.

It just so happened that we were passing over an abandoned oil exploration strip that I had checked out before and knew it was still useable. I cut the power, circled down, and landed on it. With the help of the man who had gotten him by the neck, we moved him out of the plane. The other passengers sat in stunned silence. The strip was long enough that I was able to takeoff from where we had stopped. I left the guy stranded 40 miles from civilization in bear country. I finished my route and came back to collect him about two hours later. He was very glad to see me, and was willing to sit back in the center seat, and was sorry for what he had done. When we got back to Cold Bay, I told him he would have to wait overnight and fly to Port Moller the following day. I didn't say anything to anyone, figuring he had been punished enough. Besides that, I was not too sure I wanted the company or the FAA to know what I had done.

Aghileen Pinnacles

POEM: LIFE FLIGHT FROM BEAR LAKE

Flying South West at 4000 feet.
Throttle to maximum continuous power.
The medic in back does what he can
and silently motions, fly lower.

The clouds ahead, in multiple layers,
stretch out like golden braids.
Life hangs in a balance of distance and time,
and spinning turbine blades.

He's a good man living his dreams
to hunt these beautiful lands.
Now time and fate have intervened
to ruin his wonderful plans.

He's a pale face under a blanket,
On a stretcher strapped to the floor.

He's a husband, a lover, a father provider,
who might not come home anymore.

Nearing Cold Bay as the Aghileens
stood like a cathedral in the Sun.
The medic in back did all he could,
but time and distance won.

Prince Bandar Bear Hunt

Two weeks before the hunting season opened, I got a call from our company dispatcher. He wanted to know the charter rate for a Cessna Caravan flight to Don Johnson's Bear Lake Lodge. The lodge is located on the shore of the lake about one hundred miles north of Cold Bay. I figured the time and distance then quoted him our standard rate. He was surprised by how much it would cost and asked me to figure it again. He said the trip would be for a very important person, namely Prince Bandar Bin Sultan Al Saud of Saudi Arabia, the ambassador to the U.S. I asked the dispatcher if he really believed the Prince would care about the cost, as all details would doubtlessly be handled by staff and he would never see or care about the rate.

For the next three weeks, we were busy making two flights a day taking new furniture, linen, and decorations out to the lodge. We brought a lot of equipment for setting up a complete security system in and around the lodge. There were day and night cameras with a monitor so guards could view the entire area. We also took camping equipment for his guards who would be posted outside. A satellite phone was set up with a direct connection to the White House and State Department. The lodge had some workmen smoothing the short dirt runway.

The Prince wanted two Twin Otters available at all times, plus the Cessna Caravan. That way, if one had a mechanical problem, the other one could fly. So much for worrying about the cost. The

U.S. State Department supplemented the Prince's security guards with personnel from the U.S. Secret Service.

I asked Don Johnson if he thought they could get the prince a bear. He said they were encouraging a big one to hang around down at the end of the lake. I did not ask him how. The lodge was looking just perfect—the way a high class Alaskan hunting lodge should look. The bar had a large window positioned to look out over the lake and it was a spectacular view.

The big day finally arrived, and the Prince's Boeing 707 landed at Cold Bay and taxied in on our ramp. It was beautiful, all shiny and clean, looking like new. It was hunting season and hunters were walking around with rifles, so security was very tight. Our Twin Otter taxied in close so the Prince and his entourage could come down the stairs from the jet and directly enter the Otter. As soon as they were loaded, the Otter took off for Bear Lake Lodge.

I followed in the Caravan with a load of fresh produce and one of the Prince's Nubian guards. He was a tall, athletic looking black man dressed in a black uniform. He wore mirrored glasses so it was difficult to imagine what he might be thinking. He certainly was fierce looking, and probably was fierce as well. He wore a big knife on his belt and carried what looked like an Uzi submachine gun. He sat in the co-pilot seat.

The weather was marginal with clouds and some fog. The visibility was poor but not a problem as it was easy to follow the Bering Sea shoreline north to Nelson Lagoon and Port Moller. It was a route we flew almost every day. From Port Moller, we took a compass heading to Bear Lake. The lodge airstrip was next to the shoreline, so it was easy to find. When we arrived at the lake, I circled over the airstrip and out over the lake. The guard pointed down and I nodded my head. I could see that he was nervous. We made a low approach from over the lake in order to touch down right on the end. I glanced over and saw him leaning back, stiff with fright. Apparently, he was a little less fierce when landing over water onto a short airstrip.

After unloading the passenger and freight, I went into the lodge and was talking to the other pilots. As we were talking, Prince Bandar entered the room. He walked over to us and commended us on a very good flight. He was exceptionally nice and spoke to us just as any regular hunter would have done. He mentioned that he was also a pilot, and was interested in bush flying and asked us some questions about it. We liked him very much. Later, we learned that he had flown fighter jets in the Saudi Air Force.

I was on my week off when he left, and I found out that he did indeed get a very large bear. He handed out generous tips when he left but, unfortunately, I was not there to receive one.

Caravan on rafts

Chapter IV

Caravan at Aniakchak

Five years after I started flying for MarkAir Express, I was stationed at King Salmon, Alaska during the busy fishing season. It was a fun time, and we got a lot of hours landing on beaches, sand bars, tide flats, and makeshift dirt and gravel strips. I was flying a Cessna Caravan on wheels which was a wonderful plane for the type of flying we were doing. We went into places Cessna never dreamed of, often coming back covered in mud like a four wheel drive pickup. The company had them outfitted with aluminum checker plate floors and mud flaps on the main gears. One day, another pilot and I were called into the office and asked to take two Caravan's over to the mouth of the Aniakchak River, on the Pacific side of the Alaska peninsula, and pick up a group of rafters. They had been dropped off by float planes a week earlier on the lake in the Aniakchak Crater and had floated down the river. The station manager told us the beach was long and hard. He said it had been used many times and that we would not have a problem landing on it.

It was a rare blue-sky day, and the flight over the mountains was spectacular. The green, red, and yellow minerals showing in the sun along with the blue sky was a sight to behold. There were a lot of caribou that had climbed up high to get away from the hordes of mosquitos down on the tundra. When we got to the river, we saw the rafters waiting on the beach with a pile of equipment next to a stretch of beach that looked good. I planned my approach in order to touch down and stop near them. At first, all was normal for a typical beach landing, but the Caravan suddenly bogged down and stopped. No amount of power would get it to move. I radioed the other Caravan and told him not to land and to get help. I got out and borrowed a shovel from the rafters to dig out the sand from in front of the wheels, but it would still not move more than two feet. I dug some more and got driftwood sticks to make some ramps, all to no avail.

The tide was coming rapidly, and in that part of Alaska at that time of year, tides were 13 feet high. My beautiful million dollar Caravan was about to be destroyed. In desperation, I asked the float trip guide if he thought his rafts would float it. He thought they would, although it weighed over five thousand pounds. We unpacked the rafts and dragged them over to the plane. The Caravan had a belly pod that was flat on the bottom and made a good place to locate the rafts. Fortunately, the rafters had a lot of line. I found some driftwood we could lash to the rafts to hold them flat. I placed one raft under the nose, behind the nose gear, and the other one crosswise under the belly pod. The tide was already reaching the plane as we pumped up the rafts. We got the whole thing tied together with two lines we could hold onto to keep the Caravan from floating out to sea. It really helped that in that part of the coast there were no breakers, only large swells.

About that time, a dense fog rolled in which lasted for two days. There would be no help from the company. The plane floated quite nicely, which was a tremendous relief to me. There was an Air Force General and the CEO of a well-known supercomputer company on the raft trip. They helped me hold on to the plane all night to keep it from floating away. They got to talking about artificial intelligence and some theories about how the brain works. I had been reading a book by Douglas Hofstadter titled *Godel, Escher,*

Bach: An Eternal Golden Braid about AI, that was also a Pulitzer Prize winner. They had read the same book, so it made for a very interesting conversation.

We had the Caravan pulled up close to a small two foot bank at the high tide line but were unable to hold it, and when the tide went out, it was back where it started. The fog stayed all day, and it was back to holding the lines. I knew when our 737 would be flying over on the way to Dutch Harbor, so I waded out chest deep and climbed up into the Caravan. I got the radio going and called on the company frequency. They answered immediately, very surprised to hear from me. They thought the Caravan was history. I told them the Caravan was undamaged, floating on the rafts, and that I was going to need some help. At the next high tide as we got the plane up to the bank again, a strong squall tipped it so that a wingtip touched the sand. We finally got it straight. We had buried a log to wrap a line around and were able to hold it there.

The next day, the company came with a Cessna 185 equipped with large tires. They brought four strips of plywood, two feet by eight feet, a come-along, and some shovels. They also brought some food and one man pup tents with mummy sleeping bags. Two men came to help. The rafters were flown out later that day by Caravan floatplanes. The area above the tide line was hard and flat, but it was covered with driftwood and logs. After a lot of digging, pushing, running the engine, and pulling with the come-along, we finally got the Caravan safe above the tide line. There are a lot of large brown bears around there and our encounter with two of them is another story.

We spent two days carrying driftwood and rolling logs to get an area cleared 1500 feet long and 20 feet wide. It was fortunate we had used most of the fuel. The Caravan would be light with only the three of us and the rafts on board. We had enough fuel to fly the few miles along the coast to Yantarni Bay, where there was an abandoned oil exploration strip that MarkAir used to support a fishing camp. The company brought two barrels of Jet A and a transfer pump to fuel the Caravan. Then we flew it back to King Salmon. The company took it to Anchorage where they replaced the wheel bearings and the brake discs. They washed out the engine and cleaned some sand out of the wingtip, and it was good to go. We used that plane for years after its time as an amphibian. It turned out that the company had not actually used that beach before. Although I have landed on many beaches since then, I never did it with company airplanes, unless I had personal knowledge of the conditions.

Ice Again

During the winter months at King Salmon we got quite a few days of low temperatures, high winds, fog, and snow. We were well aware of the danger of icing and did our best to avoid flying when icing could occur. The Cessna 207 I had assigned to me in the winter had no anti-ice except for a heated pitot. We had been dealing with fog and low visibility all morning and conditions did not improve until noon. A large shipment of mail had been sitting for two days and the Post Office was on our backs to get it moved.

Carrying the mail is the lifeblood of the small airlines that serve the bush villages. Sometimes, we pushed the weather. The fog finally lifted and the temperature was cold enough that the moisture in the air was frozen and not sticking to the plane. I was already loaded, and when the ATIS announced a 500 foot ceiling and two miles of visibility, I took off and headed to Pilot Point. As it is only about 80 miles south on the Bering Sea coast, I made it in good time. After unloading the mail, I had our agent call King Salmon on the landline to check the weather. The report was that conditions had improved, so I departed for King Salmon.

On the way back, I noticed that the temperature outside had begun to warm up to about the freezing level. The fog began to stick on the wings and windshield. The Cessna 207 has a very poor defrost system, so I got a chart and folded it so the heat would be directed to one small area on the windshield. That way, when it came time to land, I would be able to see ahead.

About 40 miles from King Salmon, the ice began to build up rapidly and covered the windshield completely. Soon, I had to increase the power in order to maintain the 500 feet of altitude I had. The situation deteriorated quickly, and I had to go to 10 degrees of flaps and more power. I opened up the cowl flaps and added even more power. That helped for a while, but before long I had to increase my angle of attack and add even more power.

By the time I reached Five Mile Lake, the throttle was almost wide open and the prop was almost to maximum RPM. I called the tower and notified them of my situation and they cleared me to land on either runway. I considered landing on the lake, but it was covered with a foot and a half of snow, so I pressed on. By the time I got to the airport, the throttle was wide open to max power, and the prop to full RPM. The cylinder temperatures were at the red-line and I was losing 50 feet per minute of altitude. I made a shallow, perfectly coordinated turn to runway 29 and stayed centered by looking directly out the left window. At least this time, I had a wide 7,000 foot runway. I let the plane sink down, and when I was close to touchdown, I eased the power back slightly. The moment I did, the aircraft banged down hard. I had to have one of our ground crew marshal me into parking. It is amazing how much ice that airplane could carry and still fly. It was a good thing I was empty and low on fuel. This was my second serious encounter with ice, and I will see to it that it is the very last.

Almost Exhausted

In late August after the fishing season was over, things had calmed down. I had a scheduled flight for the afternoon to Pilot Point, Ugashik, and return. I had one passenger going to Pilot Point and 400 pounds of mail and freight to distribute to the villages. The weather was good and we saw a lot of caribou as we passed Fort Jensen and two large moose as we neared Pilot Point.

I dropped the passenger and mail off at Pilot Point and hopped over to Ugashik to deliver the freight. The postmaster at Pilot Point wanted me to come back and pick up a sack of mail that was not ready when I stopped the first time, so I did. After waiting fifteen minutes, the village agent came with the mail. After the usual checks of the magnetos, prop governor, and trim, I looked for traffic and rolled out on the runway for takeoff.

All was normal, and after liftoff as we neared the end of the runway about 50 feet in the air, the engine suddenly lost power. It sounded very strange. In the thousands of hours I had flown Cessna 207s, it was a sound I had never heard before. The engine was developing just enough power to keep the plane in the air. I switched mags, but that did nothing. I changed fuel tanks thinking one of the fuel lines might be partially blocked; still no help. I momentarily tried the fuel pump, but that made it worse and I lost about 20 feet.

There was a ridge ahead, and at first, I thought I would clear it, but as I came up on it, I saw I would hit just below the top. The stall warning was sounding almost continually, so I was afraid to pull up the nose. Just as I came to it, I put down full flaps and the airplane ballooned up over the ridge. I dove down the other side to regain the speed I lost and reset to 10 degrees of flaps. The ground dropped down, and I was able to gain speed and quiet the stall warner.

Once I had some breathing room, I experimented with the throttle and mixture control and gained back enough altitude to make it back and land. I got the screwdriver I always carried in my flight bag and removed the top cowl. The manifold on the right side looked discolored, and I knew what happened. I borrowed tools from the village agent and removed the muffler. Sure enough, one of the cone shaped baffles in the muffler had come adrift and nearly occluded the outlet. After a little shaking and poking with a piece of rebar, the baffle fell out on the ground. I replaced the muffler and the cowling.

On startup, the engine run-up sounded completely normal. I

took off and headed back to King Salmon. The engine had good power, and everything was completely normal. That evening, we replaced the muffler with a new one built with the same baffles. It is interesting that the engineers who designed it never considered that might happen. The 207 was checked out and signed off good to go the next day.

A Propane High

King Salmon, Alaska, is located by Bristol Bay, near the confluence of the Kvichak and the Naknek rivers. It's a hub for air commerce, especially during the summer fishing season. Set-netters along the shore of the bay catch millions of red salmon every year. King Salmon is also a place where sport fishermen, hunters going to the lodges, and tourists going to the bear viewing sites at Brooks Lake come in on jets from Anchorage.

MarkAir Express operated Cessna 207s and 208 Caravans on wheels and a Twin Otter and Turbine Beavers' on amphibious floats. Most of my flying time was in Cessna 208 Caravans on wheels. The company had them outfitted with oversized tires, mud flaps, and aluminum checker plate floors in the cabin. In addition to mail and passengers, we hauled everything from barrels of fuel to plywood, lumber, and heavy machinery. It was a fun, exciting place to be, and I liked it a lot.

One day, I was asked to take an old C-207 freight hauler out to Tony Sarp's Katmai Lodge, a luxury fishing resort on the Alagnak River, one of the premier fly fishing rivers in the world, to pick up some empty propane tanks. The weather was marginal with fog banks in several areas. On the way out to the lodge, I looked for a pack of wolves that one of the other pilots had seen a few minutes before. I circled the place but did not see them, so continued out and buzzed the runway to make sure no moose or bears were nearby, before landing at the lodge.

I parked next to the tanks, and with the help of the lodge crew,

I crammed in as many as possible, with the valve ends facing forward and strapped down with a cargo net. To carry them legally, they had to be plugged and the hazmat paperwork filled out properly. The paperwork appeared to be in order, so after checking to see if the lodge had any outgoing mail, I took off for King Salmon.

About half way back, I ran into a fog bank, and after checking around it, decided to fly up over it. At about 1800 ft., there was a loud "pop" and the cabin was almost instantly filled with a white propane vapor. I punched the master switch off as fast as possible, and opened the door window. I stuck my face as close to the window as I could but was getting very dizzy. I had to put my hand out and scoop air into my nose in order to breathe. I managed to fly the airplane and find the airport, in semi IFR conditions using the whiskey compass, even while still feeling very dizzy.

Traffic was using runway 11 that day, and I was approaching from the North so I made a straight in to the inactive 18. I was unable to notify the tower of my intentions, as I didn't want to turn the master switch on. On final approach, I pulled the mixture and made a no-flaps landing, stopping well before the intersection. My intention was to jump out on the runway and get away from the airplane; but for some strange reason I found myself on my knees just outside the door.

The tower saw the whole thing and called the airport security officer, who drove out to see what was going on. The propane tank was still hissing as he walked up. I got to my feet and staggered out of range to get some fresh air. After a few breaths, I was as good as new. When we unloaded the tanks we found that the one that had caused the trouble was marked 'defective' and the plug had not been installed. From that time on I made it my own personal rule not only to check the paperwork but also to check the hazmat material.

Later that day, when I was down at Eddie's Fireside Inn getting a cheeseburger, a friend from the control tower came in and we decided the whole incident could just be dropped.

Danger of No Smoking

The weather at King Salmon was nice for a change, and it was a relief not to have to deal with wing and engine covers. I had a large load of mail and freight to take to one of the outlying villages. I won't say which one in order to protect the identity of the individual this story is about. I was also carrying Mike.

I had carried Mike many times. He was a quiet, agreeable fellow who had always followed instructions and never raised any trouble. The Cessna 207 was pretty well-filled with mail and freight, so I let him sit in the front co-pilot seat. Before startup I repeated my standard briefing about seat belts, no smoking, door handles, and survival gear, etc. In addition, I instructed him to not touch any controls. While we taxied out, I could smell that he had been drinking, but he appeared to be sober enough to fly legally. We taxied out to the active runway, and I did the usual run-up, checking the magnetos and prop governor, flaps set and fuel to proper tank, trim set for takeoff. With clearance from the tower, we took off from runway 29 and turned south.

All went well for about twenty minutes until the effects of the booze hit him. Apparently, he had downed a large amount just before he got on. He was getting very drunk. I knew I was in for trouble but had no idea how serious the situation would become. He reached into his jacket for his cigarettes and lighter. I told him to put them away and that he could not smoke in the airplane. In about five minutes, his brain recycled and he was going to light up, so I said, "Mike, put those away, you can't smoke until we land." I could see that he was becoming angry. I had a lot of paper packages and other flammable freight in the back and a dropped cigarette or lighter could be a disaster. A few minutes later, he started to light up again and got way over in the corner where he thought I could not stop him. I reached over and took his lighter away and told him in no uncertain terms that he could not smoke. I could see that he was getting very angry and was about to swing his fist at me. I tightened my seatbelt very tight. When he launched a haymaker, I jammed forward on the controls. He flew up in his seat and his fist went over my head. This happened twice before he got the message.

We were nearing his village, so I radioed our village agent to have the VPSO meet the plane. When we landed and parked on the ramp, I got out and let the VPSO deal with him. They had a little wrestling match in the gravel. I grounded Mike for a month, and the other airline had banned him so he was stuck. Two weeks later, he called wanting to fly. We stuck to our guns and made him wait the full month. When Mike was sober, he was really a nice fellow, and he rode with me many times after that without any problem. Alcoholism is a serious issue in many of the villages, and we had to be constantly aware of it.

One day later in the year, Mike came to our office wanting to go to Dillingham on our Beechcraft 1900. He had just received his permanent fund check from the state, which is oil money distributed to Alaska residents. Mike's check amounted to more than $1000 dollars. Knowing Mike's problem with alcohol, I knew his going to town with that much money would not be a good thing. A little over a week later, I came out in the morning to preflight the airplane for the day. Mike was sitting on the ground, leaning against the building. He had lost his jacket and his boots. He was shivering from the cold, and his left eye was badly damaged. He wanted to go home, but he had lost all of his money. I brought him into the office to warm up and paid the airfare to his village. I liked Mike, and even after all these years, I still wonder what has become of him.

Going to the Dogs

In the spring of King Salmon, before the ice melts on the river, they have a festival. The local watering holes are all busy with live music and food. They have sled dog races and even play golf on the river with colored golf balls. People come in from Naknek and other villages, and everyone has a good time. I was sent on a charter to New Stuyahok with a 207 to pick up two villagers and a dog team. They were going to enter the races. I flew over there and taxied to the ramp where they were waiting with a sled and 13 dogs. In order to get the sled in, it had to go in upside down and backwards, with the runners straddling the pilot's head. I had to slide the pilot's seat fully forward and twist the sled this way and that in order to get it in.

With the sled finally in, they began squeezing the dogs into kennels, three or four to each plastic kennel. They were growling viciously and wanted to fight, but they were packed in too tightly to move. We were able to slide the four kennels in beside the sled, with just enough room to install the 7th seat and latch the seatbelt. After that, we had dog food, mixing pots for the dog food, and metal dishes for the dogs to eat from. Then came two large duffle bags containing clothes, dog harnesses, and who knows what else.

When it was all in, one passenger sat in the co-pilot's seat and the other squeezed into the most aft 7th seat, back by the cargo doors. It's a good thing all the other seats had been left at the hangar in King Salmon. The cargo doors would just close and lock. Fortunately, it was a short 30 minute flight. I had to worm my way into the pilot's seat and sit hunched up over the control yoke with just enough room to get full travel on the elevators. I gave my normal briefing about seat belts, no smoking, door operation, survival gear, etc. I taxied out for takeoff, and after the usual run-up, setting the flaps and trim, and checking for traffic, we were off for King Salmon.

A few minutes later, after everything was set for cruise, two of the dogs got out of their kennel and one of them managed to crawl between the sled and the cabin headliner, to a position right behind my head. It continued to growl fiercely the rest of the way. The villager in the co-pilot's seat yelled and poked at it, which made the situation worse, until I made him quit. The stench was almost unbearable and

I was thankful to land and let the cargo crew deal with it.

One of the other pilots got the honor on the return trip, which was even worse, as the sled dog driver and his helper were three sheets to the wind from indulging in the festivities. They were trying to assuage their lack of victory. There was no ramp crew on the other end to help with offloading the furry cargo.

Runway Incursion

One day, while flying the bush at King Salmon Alaska, I had a charter flight to take a Cessna 207 to Ekwok and pick up the high school basketball team and their coach and take them to Naknek where they would play a game and stay overnight. It was a decent day weather-wise, with very little wind and mostly sunny. Snow covered the ground, but it was quite warm for the time of year. Everyone was in good spirits, and there was a lot of chatter and laughter during the flight.

Five miles from Naknek, I got on the radio to check for traffic, and hearing none, I announced my intention to make a straight in to the cross runway, which was into the wind. The runway had been plowed and was in good condition with six inches of snow covering the ground on both sides. After checking for traffic again, and finding there was still none, I began my final approach. At that time, I noticed a snow machine with two riders at the far end of the strip coming down on the left, about 30 feet off to the side. I turned on my landing lights to increase my visibility.

They came on down and stopped at the approach end facing us, apparently waiting for us to land. I continued on down, preparing to land. Mixture in, prop forward, and flaps to 20. About to land, I pulled back the power and went to full flaps. I was just starting to flare, when the snow machine began to move. It turned and crossed right in front of us. I was sure they were as good as dead. I slammed the power on and pulled as hard as I could.

To this day, I have a vivid memory of looking out the corner of the door window and seeing the left main gear flash past the rear riders head so close I thought it hit. Amazingly, the prop, nose gear, main gears, and the stabilizers missed them both. I immediately had another problem. We were 40 feet in the air at an impossibly steep angle with the stall warner moaning. Somehow, I was able to get leveled off without stalling. I went around for another approach and landed. When I taxied back and stopped, they were sitting on the machine staring at us.

When I got out, I never said a word to them. I figured nothing I could say would impress them more than what had just happened. A Continental 520 at 2,750 RPM at full throttle is very loud at a hundred feet. I can't imagine what it must have been like at a few inches. Because of where they were sitting at the approach end, and because of the sight angle while we approached, apparently there was very little noticeable movement, and even with the landing lights on they did not see us coming. The sound of the snow machine must have covered the sound of the airplane. Now, under similar circumstances, I never assume anything and circle before landing.

Incidentally, the Ekwok team won.

Category III in a Cessna 207

One day in the fall of the year I was stationed at King Salmon, Alaska, my scheduled flight was a mail run to Pilot Point, then Ugashik, and return. It was a foggy morning and I waited until noon until the visibility got to a 500 foot ceiling and two miles, our company minimums. The Post Office was pressuring me to get the mail delivered, so as soon as the ATIS announced those conditions, I took off and headed for Pilot Point.

Cessna 207 N9494Mike

After delivering the freight and mail to Pilot Point, I hopped over the short distance to Ugashik to deliver some mail. I had our village agent call King Salmon on the landline to check the weather. The report was that the weather had improved. I started the engine and taxied to the runway, did the check of the magnetos and propeller, flaps to 10, trim set, fuel to the proper tank, and took off for King Salmon.

At about the half way point, as I was passing Fort Jensen, I noticed the visibility was deteriorating. 20 miles from King Salmon I dialed in the ATIS and was surprised to hear that fog had rolled in and the visibility was being reported as fog to the ground and visibility one eighth of a mile. That was way below our company minimums, so I turned back to Egegik. When I arrived there, it was completely fogged in. I called our village agent on the radio and had him call King Salmon on the landline to have the company check the weather at Dillingham, Illiamna, Port Heiden, and every village in a radius I had fuel to get to.

I had a lot of fuel because that was one of my rules when flying in the bush. All the locations were reporting fog to the ground. King

Salmon was the only place that had an ILS, good lighting, and the longest runway. So I elected to go there, enter a holding pattern, and hope the weather would improve to one-half a mile which would be legal for an ILS approach. The company checked the village locations continually, but they all stayed down, and my options were eliminated as my fuel was used up. I remained in an IFR holding pattern over Caribou Hill for over two hours. The ATIS stubbornly reported visibility was way below minimums. The tower called about every 15 minutes to check up on me, which I appreciated. They were friends of mine that I knew at King Salmon. Fuel was becoming a problem, and I finally had to declare fuel critical and asked them to vector me onto the localizer for an ILS approach to runway 21.

The 207 I was flying, N9494M, was one that I had flown for almost three years. I had number two seniority at the company and had that plane assigned to me exclusively. It was not the best looking one in the fleet, but it trimmed out perfectly and was the best flying one the company had. I loved that old plane, and I knew everything there was to know about it. I could tell what it was doing just from the sound and feel of the controls. It had good radios, localizer, glide slope, ADF, DME, and a LORAN. The GPS system we use now was still in the future.

I was familiar with the ILS at King Salmon, having used it several times. When I got to the outer marker, I announced my position and started down the glide slope. I kept those needles centered exactly. When I reached the middle marker and the missed approach point, I could see nothing but a very faint pulse from the RAIL. I continued on and soon saw a glow from the approach lights go under. I held what I had and finally saw the center line to the left. I touched down firmly and braked hard, stopping near the right edge of the runway. I got permission from the tower to do a 180, and when I got back to our ramp, I had to have our ground guys marshal me into parking. When I checked the tanks, there was about 15 minutes of fuel remaining. Later, when I was down at Eddie's Fireside having a cheeseburger, one of the tower guys came in and suggested maybe we could just forget the whole thing, and that's the last I ever heard of it.

Special Request

It was the middle of the busy summer season. The fishing at Bristol Bay was reaching its peak. We had four Caravan flights a day, flying passengers, freight and mail to the surrounding villages, and four Caravan flights a week out to Katmai Lodge on the Alagnak River. The Alagnak River is one of the premier fly fishing streams in the world. It attracts famous and wealthy people from all over. The Twin Otter on amphibian floats was busy every day taking tourists to the famous bear watching site at Brooks Lake. MarkAir had two Boeing 737 flights a day and one Lockheed Hercules freight flight per week.

We were moving a lot of people and freight. One afternoon, I had a scheduled flight to Pilot Point, Ugashik, and Egegik. There were four passengers in Pilot Point and one at Egegik that needed to get to King Salmon in order to catch the afternoon flight to Anchorage. Everything had to work just right to make the connection. I had a large load of freight and mail going out and the ground crew was so busy that I was a little late leaving King Salmon.

I left the power up high and was able to make up some time on the way to Ugashik. After unloading the mail and freight, I hopped over to Pilot Point and picked up the four passengers going to King Salmon. From there we took off for Egegik, 40 miles to the north. At that time, the runway was right in the village and we had to be very careful because the villagers had the habit of crossing the runway without looking when planes were incoming.

We landed without incident. The passenger at Egegik was a woman I had dropped off the week before. When we got to the ramp, she was not there. I waited about five minutes and was ready to start the engine and leave when one of the locals came up riding his three wheeler and said, "She is down at that grey house;

I'll go and get her." He rode down and went inside. After a minute, he came riding back to where we were waiting and announced to us and the whole world, "She's getting laid, can you wait 30 minutes?" We left as soon as I could get the engine started and headed for King Salmon. When we were five miles out, I saw the 737 landing. We arrived in time for my passengers to make their connection to Anchorage.

Crash at King Salmon

The last year I flew commercially, I was working for a small Part 135 airline called Yute Air. They had a maintenance hangar at Dillingham, Alaska, where they repaired and serviced several Cessna 207s. They also had a Cessna 206 on floats and several Fairchild Metros that they used to carry passengers and freight from Anchorage to hub villages in the state.

Since I was familiar with King Salmon and all the surrounding villages, they stationed me there with one Cessna 207. The particular plane depended on the service rotation, and I had a different 207 about every three weeks. One morning, I rode the Metro out from Anchorage after my week off. When we landed at King Salmon, I was disappointed to see the dodgiest one in the fleet sitting on the ramp. It would be my mount for the next three weeks.

It had a ratty interior, scratched, faded paint, and mediocre avionics. It had over 25,000 hours total time and had spent its life pounding over rough, gravel strips. The tops of the wings had several patches where the skin had cracked as a result of all those hard landings and flight loads. It was out of rig and would not trim out correctly. I looked over the logbooks and saw they had changed out the engine the night before, and installed a used engine that still had 200 hours left before TBO, time before overhaul. It was one they had laying around the shop. They finished the installation overnight and the only test flight was a short hop from Dillingham.

The pilot that flew it to King Salmon had caught the Metro I had come in on back to Dillingham. As I checked out the old 207, N1763U, I noticed that one of the main gear tires had a large flat spot and the brake pads were worn down very badly. On startup, I also noticed the mixture control did not go clear to the panel but figured they had not adjusted it correctly when they had installed the engine. Someone had installed a standby vacuum system which was good, but they left the control hanging from the bottom of the instrument panel. Not so good. I remember thinking that if one crashed, the control would get the pilot right in the knee. I thought of the good old days at MarkAir and the beautiful Cessna Caravans I flew for them.

I flew the morning schedule down to Egegik, Pilot Point, and Ugashik, and then a turnaround back to Ugashik with more freight. I picked up a young girl who was on her way to school in Anchorage after a summer at the village. For the afternoon schedule, I had a 700 pound load of soda pop and canned goods to Coffee Point, which was located near the shore of Bristol Bay across the river from Egegik.

While we were loading the freight, I remarked to the station manager about the squealing brakes and the general worn condition of the plane. I told him, "This thing is an accident waiting to happen, and the old dog is liable to get me yet."

I filled the tanks with as much fuel as I could, given the load and the poor runway conditions at Coffee Point. The tower cleared me for takeoff on runway 29. I turned south and climbed to about 700 feet. After a few minutes, I began to adjust the mixture for cruise. I was looking out the side at some caribou and when I glanced over to check the fuel flow, I saw that nothing was happening. It became apparent that the mixture control cable had become detached.

I began a gentle turn back to King Salmon and in the middle of the turn, the engine idled back to 15 inches of manifold pressure and then to idle power. There was nothing I could do to correct the situation. I was still on the tower frequency and I could hear them giving an IFR clearance to a Northern Air Cargo DC-6 going back to Anchorage. An off airport landing was imminent, so I called Mayday, and told them I had a failed engine and would not be able to make the airport. The tower asked me my location and the number of souls on board. I told them I was solo, about six miles due south. About that time, a helicopter came up on frequency and said he was 20 miles south and would come as soon as he could. I looked for a place to set down, but there was nothing good. The tundra was very rough with big humps in all directions.

I pulled my seatbelt as tight as possible, and thanked God the little school girl was not onboard. I got the flaps down and lined up on the top of a large hump. The engine was still developing a small amount of power and I would hit on the top of the biggest one, right where I wanted to. Unfortunately, the engine quit completely just before the hump and the poor old soldier stalled, and I hit just below the leading edge of the hump.

There was a tremendous jolt.

The airplane flipped over and I went from 65 knots to zero in about 35 feet.

The cockpit filled with smoke.

I turned everything off and unsnapped my seatbelt. After falling against the headliner, I tried the door. The door would not open, so I kicked it open and slid out on the wing. I got away from the wreck, but there was no fire. It turned out, the smoke was from some engine oil that had spilled on the manifold when the propeller broke off.

The nose gear and the left main gear were torn off, and almost every piece of metal on the plane was bent. I was always good about tying down loads and had secured the 700 pounds of freight with a cargo net. I am amazed that the two small eye bolts near the back bulkhead where the net was attached did not fail. I got out of the deal with a very sore knee and some chipped teeth.

The helicopter landed about five minutes later. He had a full load of passengers, so I told him I was okay, and asked him to let the company know the coordinates where I was located. The swarms of mosquitos were unbearable, so I climbed back into the wreck. The 207 carried survival equipment in the nose compartment that included mosquito netting and repellant, but could not be accessed due to nose damage.

When I got back and walked into the office, a state trooper was there asking a lot of questions and standing close to smell if I had been drinking, which of course I had not. After that, the NTSB was on the phone asking more questions. I told them I knew exactly what happened, the mixture control had come loose. They didn't seem to believe me, but the next day when they flew out to examine the wreck, they found it was true. Three days later, after a trip to Anchorage for a drug test, a dental appointment, and an interview with the FAA, I was back in King Salmon flying 207s.

I wrote a letter to the FAA suggesting that a small, weak spring be fastened to the mixture control so if the cable became detached, the mixture would go to full rich, but I never got a reply.

Taylorcraft Restoration

At King Salmon, during the commercial and sport fishing season, our operations went almost 24 hours a day under the midnight sun. The floatplanes were busy taking tourists to the bear watching site at Brooks Lake, and the wheel planes were busy with the regular schedule, plus the flights out to fishing camps. It was a fun time of year, when we got a lot of off-airport landings. The pay was good as well because of the flying hours.

In the fall, we were busy flying hunters out to the lodges and camps for caribou, moose, and bear hunting seasons. One day, I was delivering mail to Levelock and happened to hear about a little Taylorcraft airplane stored in a building down near the river. It needed a complete rebuild, but it was complete with a low-time engine. The owner wanted to sell it, so I bought it for $1,200 dollars. I paid another villager who had a boat $300 to bring it down to the dock at Naknek.

Neil and Mike Bergt, who owned MarkAir, were kind enough to let me keep my little Piper Vagabond in their hangar and also to use some space to rebuild the Taylorcraft. I had a nice apartment over the hanger. During the winter months, the company kept one Cessna 207 to fly passengers, freight, and mail to the surrounding villages. Although there was plenty of work flying during the day, the long winter nights allowed time to work on the plane.

Five runout engines came with the plane, and I sold two of them for $800, so I was only in it for $700. I later sold a spare propeller that came with it for $700, so in the end, I had it for free. Of course, I had to buy all the materials to rebuild it.

The wings had good ribs but the spars were bad. I found a set of wings in King Salmon that had bent up ribs but the spars were good—so I had enough parts to build up a nice set of wings. All the tubing was good, so I cleaned it and gave it a coat of epoxy primer. I welded on new axles and mounted some Tri-Pacer wheels with hydraulic brakes to replace the old heel brakes with toe brakes. I got an STC from a friend to install a skylight, which really opened up the cabin. The second set of wings came with a wing tank, so I installed that with the plumbing to connect it to the main nose tank too.

One day, while I was in Anchorage, I went into Reeves' aircraft parts store and found a brand new nose cowling that had been on their shelf for many years. After I had installed new floorboards, a new windshield, new side windows, a new baggage compartment, and new fabric and paint, it was beautiful. It flew like a little feather. Early in the spring, I needed to move it out of the hangar, so on my week off, I made plans to fly it to my home on Mirror Lake, near Anchorage.

The sky was clear but the weather was cold—10 degrees below zero. I dressed up in my snow machine suit and headed for Illiamna. I topped off the nose tank and the wing tank and took off for Lake Clark Pass. The pass was clear, and the mountains and glaciers were spectacularly stunning. I made the turn where the pass narrows down and then came out at the forelands. I turned north up Cook Inlet toward Anchorage. Except for the fact that I was getting cold because there was no heat, things were going well.

It was getting a little late, but I thought I would be able to make it home before dark. I was coming up on the Beluga Natural Gas Plant when I decided to drain the wing tank into the nose tank. Unfortunately, the fuel would not transfer. Apparently a small amount of water had frozen in the line, and I would not have enough gas available to make it. The Beluga airstrip is not a public airstrip, but I figured any port in a storm, so I landed there.

Taylorcraft N33942

It was going to be too dark to continue because the Taylorcraft had no electrical system. The crew at the airstrip was very welcoming. They fed me a big dinner at the mess hall and put me up for the night. Early the next morning, they came with a big heater and warmed the whole airplane up nice and toasty. I filled up with fuel and tried to pay for the fuel, room, and board, but they refused and sent me on my way. The true Alaskan spirit! I ran into a few snow showers but made it home in good shape.

I never advertised the Taylorcraft, but a fellow saw it at Birchwood airport and offered me $12,500 for it, so I sold it. I wish now that I had kept it. Of course, I think that about every airplane I ever owned. All 20 of them.

Evans Mosquito

In 1998, I was stationed out at King Salmon, Alaska flying the bush. During the long winter nights and weekends without much to do, I decided to build an airplane similar to one I had built in 1971. I already owned an engine, prop, wheels, brakes, and other miscellaneous parts, and one of the villagers had a set of Luscombe rag wings that had been damaged on the butt ends. I wanted to shorten them by removing one bay anyway, so I bought them for a very reasonable price.

Evans Mosquito in farm hangar

The plane was my own design, influenced by those of Les Long and Tom Story. The fuselage was welded 4130. The tail surfaces and landing gear were similar to J-3 Cub construction. All bolts, pulleys, cables, turnbuckles, etc. were aircraft quality. The fabric was done using the Stits process. The project was completed and assembled in four and one half months. I called it the Mosquito.

In the year 2000, I retired from flying the bush in Alaska and moved to a small farm in Oregon. My wife, who is also a pilot, and I built a nice hangar and put in a 1,000 ft. airstrip where we kept a C-150 and a Piper Vagabond.

I shipped the Mosquito to Oregon in a container and reassembled it in the new hangar. The plane flew very nicely, cruising 105 mph at 2250 rpm. It got off in 300 ft., landed in less than 500 ft., and stalled very gently at around 40 mph indicated.

I flew it about 15 hours during the test phase and had it parked in an open "T" hangar. Two of the neighbor's large dogs chased a squirrel into an open inspection plate hole and proceeded to rip the wing to shreds. I was not mad at the dogs. They were nice, just doing what dogs do. I disassembled the plane and put it in dry storage where it remained for 17 years.

We sold the farm, so I got the Mosquito out and repaired the wing in order to move it to our new home. I will fly the rest of the 40 hour test phase as weather permits.

Engine: Lyc. 0-145 65 HP
Empty Wt: 525 lbs.
Wing span: 27' 6"
Length: 17' 7"
Cruise: 105 mph
Top speed: 115 mph
Stall: 40 mph

MY 10 RULES FOR FLYING THE BUSH

- If there is any doubt of the outcome of an operation, then you do not do it.

- Never let the airplane fly you. You make it do what it is capable of.

- Always carry as much fuel as possible considering the load and landing area.

- When flying along a shoreline in poor visibility, always leave room to reverse course by turning toward the shoreline.

- When operating on a beach or sandbar, always make turns uphill.

- Never let passengers pressure you into anything.

- If something is distracting you, slow down and go by the checklist.

- Always know how the plane is loaded and tie down the load.

- Never assume anything.

- Always be friendly to your competition, and never hesitate to help them with flight safety information.

Glossary

ADF – Automatic Direction Finder

Aileron – A hinged surface in the trailing edge of an airplane wing, used to control lateral balance

Alaska Permanent Fund Dividend – A dividend paid to Alaska residents that have lived within the state for a full calendar year

ATIS – Automatic Terminal Information Service, provides meteorological information

AWOS – Automatic Weather Observing System

Belly Pod – A container attached to the aircraft underside to store cargo or fuel

CAVU – Ceiling and Visibility Unlimited

CIA – Cook Inlet Aviation

Control Zone – A volume of airspace around an airport from the ground to a specified upper limit

DME – Distance Measuring Equipment

GCA – Ground Controlled Approach to landing

GPS – Global Positioning System

Holding Patterns – The way an aircraft circles in a designated airspace to delay its descent to the runway

IFR – Instrument Flight Rules

ILS – Instrument Landing System

Jet A – A kerosine grade of fuel suitable for most turbine-engined aircraft

Localizer – A system of horizontal guidance in the Instrument Landing System

LORAN – Long Range Navigation system using low frequency radio waves

Magnetos (Mags) – An electrical generator which use magnets to ignite an engine via sparkplugs, piston aircraft engines have two

Master Switch – A switch that powers up all the aircraft systems

Minimums – Weather minimum limits relating to visibility and cloud cover for flying

Nose Gear – The front wheel that supports the nose of the aircraft on landing

NTSB – National Transportation Safety Board

Outer Marker – A white beacon light that lines pilots up to the center of the runway during initial approach

Part 135 – Federal regulations for non-scheduled commercial operations for air charters and air taxi flights

Pitot Tube – A slender tube mounted on the wing that measures air speed

Prop Governor – A device that automatically adjusts the angle of an aircraft's propeller

Radar – Monitors an aircraft's descent angle and course for landing

RAIL – Runway Alignment Indicator Lights that help the pilot align with the runway center line

Special VFR Clearance – Allows pilots to fly in weather conditions that are below standard Visual Flight Rules' minimums

STC – Supplemental Type Certificate. A certificate issued by the FAA which allows a modification to an aircraft part.

Trim – An adjustable device that can hold the airplane steady for straight and level flight

VPSO – Village Public Safety Officer

As far back as he can remember, Gary was always interested in things that flew. Like many young boys, he built model airplanes while growing up. He began taking flying lessons while still in high school from a wonderful lady named Arlene Baker, who had been a WAAF pilot during WW II. He was drafted into the army one month after graduating, before he could get his pilot's license. His flying was delayed by two years in the Army and then college, where he earned a BA in biology with a minor in chemistry.

While working for a pharmaceutical company he completed his flying lessons and obtained his pilot's license. Over the next several years he built a homebuilt airplane of his own design and restored several other classic factory built aircraft.

Upon moving from Oregon to Anchorage, Alaska, he started a small general contracting business, and obtained a commercial license with multi-engine and instrument ratings. He met and married his wife who was a private pilot and also appreciated airplanes and equipment.

www.ingramcontent.com/pod-product-compliance
Lightning Source LLC
LaVergne TN
LVHW031541060526
838200LV00056B/4593